3 0063 00358 2519

 Fairmount   Oct 2020

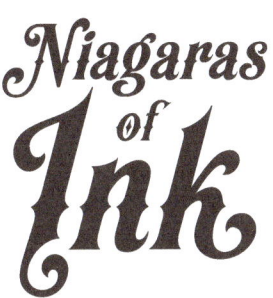

DAVENPORT PUBLIC LIBRARY
321 MAIN STREET
DAVENPORT, IOWA 52801-1490

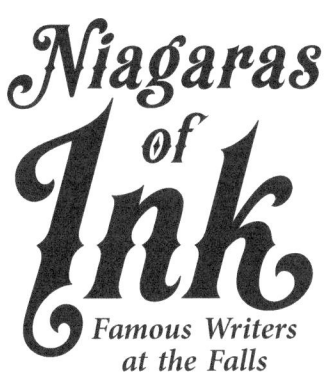

Niagaras of Ink
Famous Writers at the Falls

Jamie M. Carr

excelsior editions
AN IMPRINT OF STATE UNIVERSITY OF NEW YORK PRESS

Cover: *Rarer Views*, Stereoscope, Box SV-55, Niagara Falls Public Library, NY.

Back cover: *Scene of the Late Casualty—Niagara Falls. The Illustrated News*, August 06, 1853, Issue 32, p. 1.

Published by State University of New York Press, Albany

© 2020 State University of New York

All rights reserved

Printed in the United States of America

No part of this book may be used or reproduced in any manner whatsoever without written permission. No part of this book may be stored in a retrieval system or transmitted in any form or by any means including electronic, electrostatic, magnetic tape, mechanical, photocopying, recording, or otherwise without the prior permission in writing of the publisher.

Excelsior Editions is an imprint of State University of New York Press

For information, contact State University of New York Press, Albany, NY
www.sunypress.edu

Library of Congress Cataloging-in-Publication Data

Names: Carr, Jamie M., 1971– author.
Title: Niagaras of ink : famous writers at the Falls / Jamie M. Carr.
Description: Albany : State University of New York Press, [2020] | Series: Excelsior editions | Includes bibliographical references and index.
Identifiers: LCCN 2019040800 | ISBN 9781438479989 (pbk. : alk. paper) | ISBN 9781438479996 (ebook)
Subjects: LCSH: Niagara Falls (N.Y. and Ont.)—In literature. | American literature—History and criticism. | English literature—History and criticism. | Authors, American—Travel—Niagara Falls (N.Y. and Ont.) | Authors, English—Travel—Niagara Falls (N.Y. and Ont.) | Niagara Falls (N.Y. and Ont.)—Description and travel.
Classification: LCC PS169.N53 C37 2020 | DDC 810.9/971339—dc23
LC record available at https://lccn.loc.gov/2019040800

10 9 8 7 6 5 4 3 2 1

For Grace, my own natural wonder

What poets shed from countless quills, Niagaras of ink . . .

—Col. Peter A. Porter, in *Niagara:
Its 1872 History and Geology, Incidents and Poetry*

Contents

List of Illustrations	xi
Prologue: Seeing Niagara with Different Eyes	xiii
Acknowledgments	xv
Introduction: Lost Pages	1
Chapter 1 Old Worlds, New Voices	9
Chapter 2 Clean Water and Clean Air	27
Chapter 3 The Falls and Fame	41
Chapter 4 Copyrights and Wrongs	55
Chapter 5 Books That Started a War	75
Chapter 6 Bridge Traffic	85
Chapter 7 Words of Art	97
Chapter 8 War, and Peace	111
Chapter 9 Case Closed?	123
Chapter 10 Save Niagara	141
Epilogue: Still Seeing Niagara	149

Notes	151
Works Cited	171
Index	185

Illustrations

Figure 1	Arthur Lumley (Irish, c. 1837–1912). *Niagara Seen with Different Eyes*, 1873.	xiii
Figure 2	Ralph Waldo Emerson's signature, Bath Island Register, January 4, 1863.	2
Figure 3	"The American House," *Winchester Daily Bulletin*, Winchester, Tennessee, February 10, 1863.	3
Figure 4	Margaret Fuller's Cataract House Hotel registration, May 28, 1843.	20
Figure 5	Sketch reproduced from *Washington Irving: Journals and Notebooks*, vol. 5, *1832–1859*.	32
Figure 6	Henry David Thoreau Herbarium, Goat Island plant pressing.	36
Figure 7	Henry David Thoreau Herbarium, Goat Island plant pressing.	37
Figure 8	H. W. Longfellow family and friends at Niagara Falls.	39
Figure 9	Nathaniel Hawthorne's printed certificate to Niagara Falls (Termination Rock) from 1832.	47
Figure 10	Advertisement, *Buffalo Evening News*, January 31, 1882, to April 27, 1882.	51
Figure 11	"An Exaggerated Niagara," published in Twain's travel book *Following the Equator: A Journey around the World*, 1897.	66

Figure 12	Thomas Nast, "Innocence Abroad (in search of a copyright)," *Harper's Weekly*, January 21, 1882.	69
Figure 13	"Walt Whitman on Seeing Niagara," *Newtown Bee*, Newtown, Connecticut, 1877.	95
Figure 14	William Dean Howells's Cataract House Hotel registration, July 17, 1860.	99
Figure 15	Henry James's Cataract House Hotel registration, September 25, 1871.	107
Figure 16	"Lady Conan Doyle 'Lost' Six Hours," *Buffalo Courier*, April 27, 1922, to May 21, 1922.	127
Figure 17	"Even 'Sherlock Holmes' Fails to Find Lost Wife and Children," *Evening World*, May 12, 1922.	128
Figure 18	"Wife of Author Rests Quietly at Niagara Falls, Ont., Hotel," *Buffalo Courier*, April 27, 1922, to May 21, 1922.	129
Figure 19	Original photograph published in Jack London's *The Road*. New York, Macmillan, 1907.	135
Figure 20	Original photograph published in London's *The Road*. New York, Macmillan, 1907.	136
Figure 21	H. G. Wells's "The End of Niagara," *Harper's Weekly*, Saturday, July 21, 1906.	145

Prologue

Seeing Niagara with Different Eyes

𝒜 single illustration of Niagara Falls might be said to best capture the contested history of its landscape and the many perspectives that have shaped its meaning over time. Published in *Harper's Weekly* in 1873 by Irish-American artist Arthur Lumley,[1] *Niagara Seen with Different Eyes* (see figure 1) invites the viewer to look at others looking—to see the Falls

Figure 1. Arthur Lumley (Irish, c. 1837–1912). *Niagara Seen with Different Eyes*, 1873, wood engraving, 15½ × 21¾ in., Collection of the Castellani Art Museum of Niagara University, Generous Donation from Dr. Charles Rand Penney, partially funded by the Castellani Purchase Fund, with additional funding from Mr. and Mrs. Thomas A. Lytle, 2006.

through the eyes of soldier and sailor, poet and painter, businessman and patriot. We perceive the conflicting views foregrounded by the figures of "Uncle Sam" and in the romanticized image of indigenous people. We sense the contrast between feeling—sentiment, love, and spirit—and utilitarianism—territory, tourism, and industry. As we cast our eye across the scene, we notice the movement of the water and of the mist, of the traveler, and of time. And though we are given a glimpse of individuals at an iconic place in a single moment of their lives, their personal stories are not visible.

Lumley presents these figures as "types" to convey predominant ways the Falls have been approached across time. If we are meant to understand something of what drew each to the Falls, we are left to ask: Who is it that visited, and when? How did they travel? What did they see and do? And most of all, what did they think about their experiences? In many ways the figures in Lumley's illustration represent the writers foregrounded in this book—writers who traveled to the Falls as tourists; who set out to make a living; to immerse themselves in nature; to characterize or critique the landscape; who journeyed for freedom; writers in short, who sought meaning in the Falls. This book uncovers what happened when they arrived.

Acknowledgments

What is it that makes us feel connected to certain places? When I returned to New York State, just over a decade ago and was new to the Niagara region, I hadn't yet felt a connection to it as I did to places more familiar to me, like the Adirondacks, where I spent childhood summers revisiting the sites of my mother's youth. Then one day, a colleague shared with me an article her father had written on Oscar Wilde at Niagara Falls.

For years, while I was busy with the demands of a new academic job and working toward tenure, Wilde's visit remained in the back of my mind. One story soon turned into many stories. The more I read and researched the writers included in this collection, the more thoroughly I came to appreciate Niagara Falls and the belief that literature and knowledge of others' experiences—that is to say, stories—can shape our relations to places.

I thank fellow Wilde enthusiasts, Amelia Gallagher and Bill Gallagher, for sharing a story. I am also deeply indebted to several friends and colleagues for their thoughtful feedback and endless support of this book, especially Sarah Holmes and Robert St. Hilaire. The expertise of Paula Kot and Eric Purchase, and peer reviewers for SUNY Press, likewise helped to make this a better book. My editors at SUNY Press, Amanda Lanne-Camilli and Jenn Bennett-Genthner, provided patience as well as guidance, for which I am very appreciative. Carrie Teresa and Doug DeCroix were generous with their time as well. Thank you to Sara Anderson for careful work on the index. Any errors throughout are, of course, my own.

The research for this book often felt unwieldy, and I am grateful to have had assistance at various institutions, from a number of people, especially Local History Librarian Courtney Geerhart, and clerk Helga

Schultz, Niagara Falls Public Library. David Schoen, director, and Samantha Gust, head of acquisitions, at the Niagara University Library, as well as Mary Helen Miskuly, registrar, at the Castellani Art Museum at Niagara University, made sure I had access to requested materials; Tom Collister, curator of the Historical Association of Lewiston, provided assistance with a Frontier House question; and the librarians at the New York Public Library, the Henry W. and Albert A. Berg Collection of English and American Literature, and the Brooke Russell Astor Reading Room for Rare Books and Manuscripts, were helpful in my review of the papers of Rupert Brooke and of Washington Irving.

Further, the following libraries, archives, and museums generously provided assistance and granted permissions to reproduce material: Niagara Falls Public Library; New York State Library; Harvard University Herbaria; Longfellow House–Washington's Headquarters National Historic Site; Beinecke Rare Book and Manuscript Library, Yale University; Castellani Art Museum, Niagara University; and the Niagara University Library. The Niagara University Research Council provided generous support for this project. Databases that preserve documents of the past and make them widely accessible have been indispensable, including: the Nineteenth-Century US Newspapers Database and ProQuest Historical Newspapers: the *New York Times*, both made available through my University library; the Library of Congress Prints and Photographs Division; Ancestry.com; Chronicling America; HathiTrust Digital Library; and Documenting the American South (University of North Carolina at Chapel Hill Library); Fulton Search: Historic Newspapers; among others.

I was fortunate throughout much of this project to have shared a three-year-long interdisciplinary "Discover Niagara" project with colleagues Bill Cliff and Paula Kot. Thanks to both, and to Tom Chambers, for sharing their disciplinary insights on the Falls. The Castellani Art Museum was always welcoming with its vast collection of Niagara Falls images. Thanks to Michael Beam, for early support on the Oscar Wilde trail, and Tara Walker for facilitating student visits to the museum. My students in "Literary Niagara" deserve a huge note of thanks for humoring me. And thank you to Brian Bennett for sharing Writer's Tears.

I am indebted to so many whose interest in the project helped to keep me writing. Such thanks to my family, especially my parents, Jim and Mary, who gave me my first sense of place. And most of all, to Ed and Grace, who toured sites with me, accompanied me on research trips, and gave me feedback and support whenever I lost direction.

Citations in this volume appear in Robert Price, ed., "The Road to Boston: 1860 Travel Correspondence of William Dean Howells," *Ohio History* 80 (Spring 1971): 85–154. Courtesy of the Ohio History Connection.

Introduction

Lost Pages

Ralph Waldo Emerson:
The Value of What Has Been Lost

(1803–1882)

On his third visit to Niagara Falls in 1863, Ralph Waldo Emerson admired its "immense plenty." Today, this visit represents all that might have been lost.

The prominent American essayist and poet Ralph Waldo Emerson made it a point to visit Niagara Falls while on speaking tours to neighboring cities beginning in the 1850s. When he arrived for his third time at the Falls on January 4, 1863, he was inspired anew for, "its immense plenty." "The vast quantity of water that pours over it in five minutes suggests the huge continent from which it draws its supplies," he wrote in a letter to his daughter.[1] North America—and more likely in Emerson's view, America—symbolically lent Niagara Falls its vast power, even if, in 1863, it was a nation divided.

The start of 1863 was promising. President Abraham Lincoln signed the Emancipation Proclamation on the first of that new year. To celebrate, Emerson read his "Boston Hymn" to a New England audience: "To-day unbind the captive, / So only are ye unbound," he declared. The call was clear: "unchain the slave:" so that "Free be his heart and hand henceforth / As wind and wandering wave."[2] American freedom should mean freedom for all.

After delivering his poem, Emerson left for a western lecture tour. As print production and literacy increased in the nineteenth century, a reading public emerged, one interested in learning but typically without access to formal education. Popular lectures often filled this gap. Taking a short break from his lecture tour, Emerson stopped off at Niagara Falls, touring the American side. He signed his name in the Bath Island Register (now Green Island), where he likely paid a toll to cross the bridge to Goat Island to take in the views. (See figure 2.) Emerson's reference to that "vast quantity of water" suggests that the Falls were not fully frozen at the

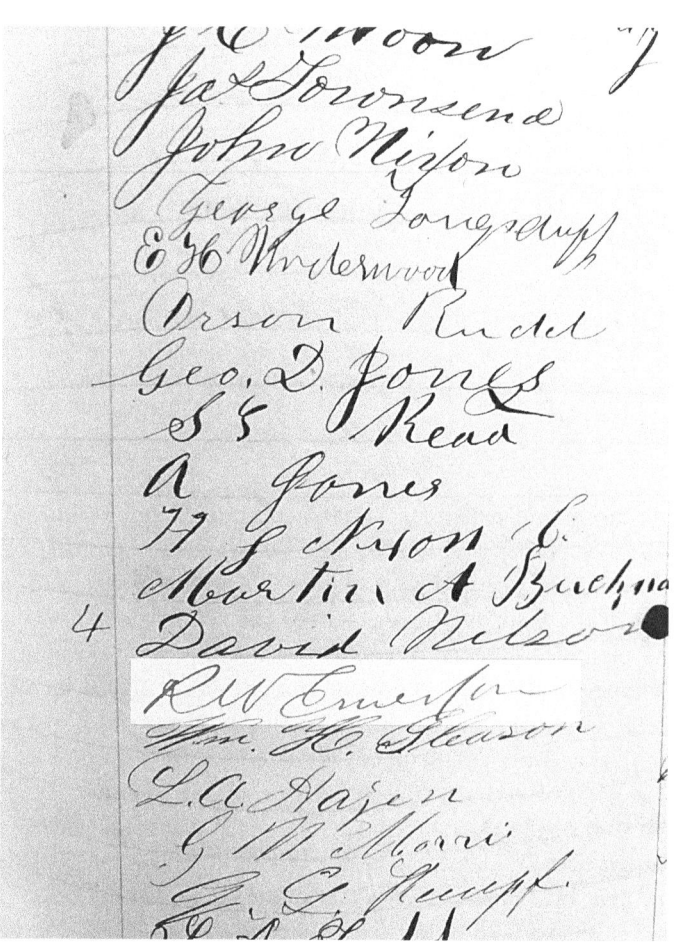

Figure 2. Ralph Waldo Emerson's signature on January 4, 1863. Bath Island Register, August 6, 1862 to August 8, 1863. Niagara Falls Public Library.

time of his early January visit. Still, winter travel from New England to Western New York may not have been without hazard and a good night's rest was in order. Emerson checked into the American House hotel, "the only hotel open in winter," and had gone to bed early.

At 3:00 a.m., shouts of "Fire!" sounded alarm through the house. The sense of panic that ensued is conveyed in the breathless, rushed way Emerson recites the night's events to his daughter Edith, even from the safety of the Eagle Hotel in Rochester, New York three days later:

> I put on my clothes or some of them, & gathered up my properties as many & as fast as I could in the dark, & got down stairs through a cloud of smoke & cinders, and found women clothed in blankets & barefooted in the hall & in the street, & great distress everywhere. The house was burned out thoroughly, before all our eyes, & nothing left but the four walls. All the furniture, & quantities of clothing, & much money of the guests & of the proprietor, were lost. I had left my baggage at the Suspension Bridge, & had with me only my black-bag; but contrived to lose my ticket from Buffalo to Chicago, and some brushes, &c. no insurance.[3]

The local newspaper, the *Niagara Gazette* reported that the fire "spread with such fearful rapidity to the main building that the halls and rooms were filled with smoke before any general alarm was given."[4] Though Emerson's experience was briefly cited in American newspapers over the subsequent week, none would convey the enormity of his survival. (See figure 3.)

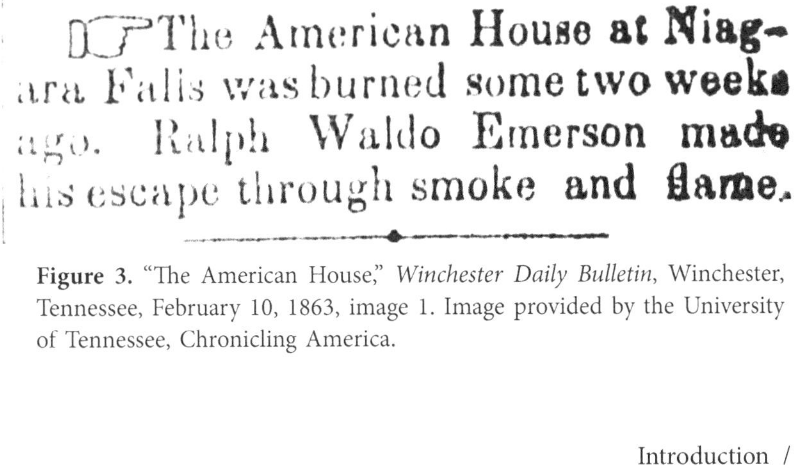

> ☞The American House at Niagara Falls was burned some two weeks ago. Ralph Waldo Emerson made his escape through smoke and flame.

Figure 3. "The American House," *Winchester Daily Bulletin*, Winchester, Tennessee, February 10, 1863, image 1. Image provided by the University of Tennessee, Chronicling America.

Upon his escape, Emerson walked two miles to the Niagara Suspension Bridge.[5] With good fortune, he ran into the superintendent of the Michigan Central Railroad, whom Emerson knew from Concord, Massachusetts, and, "as if posted at the bridge by special act of providence, he insisted on giving Emerson a pass from Detroit to Chicago, thus saving him a large part of the expense of replacing the lost ticket."[6]

It might be said that the proverbial third time had worked its charm for Emerson—and for Niagara Falls, which did not earn the dubious distinction of causing the death of one of the most renowned nineteenth-century American literary celebrities.[7] Emerson survived. But, his and others' losses were notable. Of the American Hotel, as Emerson put it, there was "nothing left."

Recovery

Not surprisingly, the headlines that dominated the Wednesday morning, January 7, 1863 edition of the *Niagara Gazette* were the national and local news stories cited above: "Proclamation by the President of the United States of America" and, in "Local and Vicinity News," the "Burning of the American Hotel."[8] Emerson is not mentioned, however, and so he and Niagara Falls went their separate ways in the historical archives.

What *is* surprising is that Emerson, who wrote about the importance of nature to the mind and spirit, did not publish work explicitly on Niagara Falls. But others did. Many others. The Falls tested the powers of description. From the sublime to the satirical, writers observed the landscape in all its facets, from the awe inspiring to the disappointing. Among the most notable visitors who continue to garner attention today are Anthony Trollope, Charles Dickens, Nathaniel Hawthorne, Oscar Wilde, and Mark Twain. Little has been written, however, of less "sublime" moments famous writers encountered—like Emerson's hotel fire—which nevertheless add richness to the region's sense of place.

Since the early nineteenth century, writers went to the Falls as tourists and as travelers. Most went to make a living by writing travel essays. A rising middle class with the money and leisure to travel could do so more easily thanks to evolving technologies of mobility—the stagecoach, canal, steamboat, and railroad. Innovations in printing and papermaking contributed to increases in print material and in literacy rates. Guidebooks and periodicals that printed travel essays proliferated. Landscape tourism was on the rise, and Niagara Falls was an obvious draw, with its picturesque views and promise of sublime experiences.

Sometimes writers stayed only a day or two, long enough to note their impressions in a "letter" to be published in daily newspapers. Others immersed themselves for a week or longer to try to capture the spirit of the place, what Oscar Wilde referred to as the "feeling of sublimity"—of awe and transcendence—the many guidebooks and other travel writers promised. It might be said that Niagara made writers of tourists and tourists of writers.[9] But not all who came to Niagara were so privileged.

The Niagara River and its surrounding lands were long a site and source of livelihood, travel, and trade for indigenous people before and after settler wars and international borders carved up traditional territories. For fugitive slaves, the border was both a place of promise and peril. A site of conflict and of peace, the Falls have long been a symbol of cultural and personal significance for indigenous, refugees and for pilgrims from of all walks of life.

A century ago, the once-commissioner of the State Reservation at Niagara, Charles Mason Dow, undertook a monumental task—to compose a comprehensive bibliography of writings on Niagara Falls. Dow "could not help feeling," he explains in 1917, "that very few of the millions who make their hurried pilgrimage to the wonder of the western world . . . ever dream how fascinating and old and vast the literature of the Falls is." Dow's solution was to compile this vast material in one place, in "a bibliography and anthology of the Falls." At the very least, he wanted to convey "some slight idea of the great extent of Niagara literature."[10] In the days before digitization and accessibility to manuscripts and other ephemera, Dow's bibliography was no small achievement—1,400 pages across two volumes of writing in history, geography, botany, literature, music, and more. The more well-known of these impressions of the Falls continue to be cited in local histories and in tourist guidebooks. Additionally, the newly established Niagara Falls Underground Railroad Heritage Center near the site of the former Suspension Bridge brings to life the stories of freedom seekers and abolitionists, including Harriet Tubman and the Rev. Josiah Henson, whose narratives are included in this present collection.

Still, the vast *literary* heritage of Niagara Falls remains primarily in the archives. Well-known authors from the nineteenth century who shaped national literatures, and who helped to shape the symbolic landscape of the Falls, neither lived there nor died there.[11] Though literary tourism sites exist along the Niagara frontier,[12] there are no famous writers' homes or gravesites to visit in the region of the Falls. As Emerson's experience highlights, the hotels they stayed in during their day- or weeklong visits burned down or were destroyed to make way for newer structures. No heritage museum exists to collect memories of their travels.

The sites writers visited are transformed too. The protruding Table Rock on the Canadian side of the Falls has long since crumbled into the gorge. Terrapin Tower, a stone observatory once hovering at the brink of Horseshoe Falls on the American side—a site, according to novelist and editor William Dean Howells, "where half the civilized world has inscribed its names, in different styles of character, on the walls"—was blown up and has been replaced by a concrete outcrop and railings.[13] Biddle Stairs, which led down into the gorge from Goat Island, was destroyed in 1927, two years after an elevator was installed to provide access to the Cave of the Winds.[14] Plastic ponchos rather than the oilskin capes and hats of the past are now donned at Cave of the Winds and Journey behind the Falls, on the *Maid of the Mist* and the *Hornblower*; and so much more.

Nevertheless, the writers included here stood on the brink of the gorge, descended below the Falls, saw and heard that great rush of silver-green water thunder its way over the rocky ledge, and felt the spray from its ancient pools. And though the traces are few, these exist too—signatures in hotel registers, photographs, newspaper articles, and other ephemera that writers saw or touched or wrote, gathered here for the first time.

An Anthology of Anecdotes

After four centuries of writings on the Falls, how does one make the story of Niagara new?[15] Unlike Dow's earlier work, this collection incorporates anecdotes of writers' experiences with a curated anthology of some of the most engaging Anglo-American writing on the Falls from the early nineteenth to the early twentieth centuries.[16] Included are previously untold stories, authors not included in other literary histories of the Falls, new takes on well-known material, or tales and texts just too good to exclude.

In researching the many voices included here, through the textures of events and impressions that made their way into journals and archives, old patterns surfaced, themes that travel across historical time and resonate still today: the Falls as restorative, or a business opportunity; the Falls as freedom, or a border; the Falls a work of art, or an object to be used; the Falls as a place of peace, or of conflict. Similar to Lumley's "types," I have chosen to cluster the authors around these themes, rather than to march them singularly through chronological time. But while I offer ways to approach the material included, neither chapter introductions nor author sketches can fully account for the writers' incredibly rich lives and texts or how these help to shape the meanings and uses that have been made of the Falls.

This book is not meant to provide a definitive literary legacy then, but to begin an archive of stories otherwise lost from the pages of history and to contribute to the cultural heritage of the region. Critiques may be made that the names are too traditional or that there are notable omissions. This book is neither a beginning nor an end to the literary story of Niagara Falls. But hopefully the writers selected are recognizable to a variety of readers, their stories compelling in their own contexts, and their words sympathetic to human experience, demonstrating how individual lives are intertwined with historical unfolding, connected to broader issues and events and yet uniquely particular.

The title of this book is taken from a poem by an unknown hand, however—generally unknown other than locally, that is. Col. Peter A. Porter was a descendent of a military and business family who helped to establish Niagara Falls as a place of commerce and tourism and is celebrated as a Civil War hero in his own right. But while he knew a few prominent writers and artists, and was a poet who could also sketch, he was not himself famous for these talents.[17] Still, his verse remembers a long tradition of those drawn to Niagara's brink, a history Porter understood as meaningful even by the middle of the nineteenth century. What writers "shed from countless quills"—"Niagaras of ink"—are worth revisiting today.

Chapter 1

Old Worlds, New Voices

The *literary* story of Niagara Falls tends to begin with the Recollet Franciscan priest, Fr. Louis Hennepin, who in the early 1680s penned the first known *written* account of seeing the Falls firsthand.[1] Like other Europeans before him, Hennepin described his travels as an encounter with a "New World." Printed in Europe and translated into English in 1698, his narrative was titled to convey this sense of newness and wonder: *A New Discovery of a Vast Country in America*.[2] To Hennepin and other Europeans, the land was an archetypal myth perceived both as wild and threatening but also idyllic and regenerative.[3] Of Niagara Falls, Hennepin wrote: the space "betwixt the Lake Ontario and Erie" was a "vast and prodigious Cadence of Water" that did "foam and boyl after the most hideous manner imaginable." Unlike the Old World, the Falls presented a new geography, just as the land around it necessitated new relations as Hennepin and others depended for survival on indigenous peoples long present in the region—through their knowledge of the land's resources, through trade, and through alliances. So-called discoverers, like Hennepin, sent accounts of the landscape back to the "Old World," contributing to further European expansion into North America, to adventure and travel, and to a literary industry.

Though a few presses had been brought to the New World by the time of Hennepin's visit, they primarily printed laws, sermons, and primers. Over the next several decades, newspaper publishing was on the rise, particularly in the American colonies, with nearly 200 in circulation after the Revolutionary War. Books were often imported from the Old World, though that too began to change by the late eighteenth century. After the War of 1812, commercial publishing increased, aided by the availability of presses and paper mills (including one on Bath Island at Niagara Falls in 1823), easier travel for book trade, and a growing literate public. By the early decades of the nineteenth century, women, free blacks, the formerly enslaved, and Native writers found it increasingly possible to insert their voices into the emerging literary landscape of the New World.

Travel writing afforded women an opportunity to earn their own livings, providing a means of independence, even if their travel was typically accompanied by a male relative for the assurance of respectability. For writers such as Catherine Maria Sedgwick and Margaret Fuller, travel writing provided the opportunity to write back to male-dominated views of the landscape and to critique the treatment of the land and its indigenous inhabitants.

Here was the paradox for indigenous authors—the rise in print culture in North America "worked alongside . . . more overt weapons of conquest" of Native peoples.[4] Indigenous material culture in the form of oral narratives, wampum belts, pictographic and documentary practices extended to print in English by the early nineteenth century—through the processes of colonization by white settlers and Christian missionaries. Native writers, like David Cusick (Tuscarora), nevertheless found that English could be used to write back to the dominating culture—to stake a claim to the history and knowledge of the land.

Catharine Maria Sedgwick: Captivating History

(1789–1867)

Catharine Maria Sedgwick set out on a "grand tour" from New York to Canada just as tourism at Niagara Falls became a commercial industry. Though the development of the land may have invited travelers west, it was, as Sedgwick and others well knew, at the cost of Indian removal from the landscape.

Just as the first American travel guides were published,[5] Catharine Maria Sedgwick embarked on what she called "the grand tour" from her home in Western Massachusetts to Canada in 1821. With her brother and a small group of friends, she visited the sites that would soon fill the pages of numerous guidebooks. What was coming to be known as America's Northern or "Fashionable" Tour drew those with money and leisure to travel to the Hudson River Valley, the mountainous regions of Upstate New York, and westward to Niagara Falls; its Canadian counterpart took tourists to the "Lower Canada" cities of Quebec and Montreal, and the "Upper Canada" regions of what was then Bytown (now Ottawa), Little York (Toronto), and Niagara Falls.[6] Sedgwick's work contributed to an emerging American national literature, partly shaped by her grand northern tour and her perception of this "new world."[7]

Sedgwick's travels took her first to Albany, New York and nearby Schenectady, where she could see the construction of the Erie Canal, noting that between there and Albany a thousand men were at work. In Utica, her group boarded a boat where Sedgwick was impressed by the "novelty" of the locks with their "mechanical rising and falling." As the Erie Canal was still only midway through its construction in 1821, the Sedgwick party may have taken it to as far as Montezuma, New York, before hiring a stagecoach to Batavia and then on to Buffalo. They arrived on the Canadian side of the Falls on June 30, in what was then called Stamford Village.[8]

Sedgwick's travel party stayed at William Forsyth's inn and tavern, along the upper rapids behind Horseshoe Falls. Forsyth was an audacious and dubious businessman, with a prior history of arrest and prison escape. In 1818 he built a covered stairway to below Table Rock, which tourists could use to see the Falls up close—for a small fee.[9] The year of Sedgwick's visit, he purchased more land around his inn to build the stately Pavillion Hotel in 1822. He negotiated with guides and stagecoaches to direct tourists to his establishment, drawing business away from other inns. By 1827, in competition with other hoteliers, Forsyth boarded up access to the Falls so that tourists had to pay for a view, a decision that lead to a number of court battles.

Back in 1821, however, Forsyth's inn appeared to be the place to stay. Sedgwick and group booked a guide, who was likely working for Forsyth, to take them down to the Falls. Margaret Fuller would later quip that hiring a guide at the Falls was like hiring someone to point out the moon, but the guides were likely convincing to early tourists new to the region. Soon they would become the well-known "hacks" and "touts" that many subsequent writers satirized.

Sedgwick and her companions stayed two nights at the Canadian Falls. Her journal of the visit celebrates the New World against the Old—

"the ivy-mantled towers and blasted oaks of older regions." Five years later in her 1826 short story "The Catholic Iroquois," she remarked on this old/new contrast: "People did not go about the world then, as they do now-a-days, just to look at rapids and waterfalls."[10] Sedgwick's story maps this new tourism industry at the same time that it comments on the conflicts that made land development possible.

In the story, the tale of "the Catholic Iroquois" is told to a traveler, a French gentleman, on his way from Niagara to Montreal who is unable to find a room to rent because, "Every apartment—every nook and corner was occupied by an English party, on their way to the Falls."[11] Fortunately, the traveler is led to a kindly peasant's cottage where he makes an even greater discovery of "an antique, worm-eaten, travelling portfolio" that contains the story within the story—the captivity narrative of two Iroquois girls. Sedgwick's story is based on the true tale of Iroquois sisters taken captive by French Catholics and converted, as detailed in the records of the French Jesuit priest Pierre Francois Xavier de Charlevoix who traveled the Great Lakes region in the early 1720s. Sedgwick's layered tale reframes the conventional captivity narrative, typically stories of the capture of white settlers, often women, by Indians.

It may have been Sedgwick's grand tour that inspired her to write "The Catholic Iroquois." After leaving the Falls, Sedgwick traveled to Youngstown, New York and boarded the steamboat *Ontario*.[12] There she wrote a letter home, noting her disappointment in not having met up in Oneida with a distant cousin, Eleazar Williams. Williams was a clergyman who descended from the family of Eunice Williams, who, at the age of seven, had famously been taken captive from Deerfield, Massachusetts in 1704 by a French, Mohawk, and Abenaki war party. Eunice was moved to a mission fort in Montreal where she was raised by a Mohawk Catholic family, and eventually married into the nation.

Sedgwick more explicitly revisited this family history in her popular 1827 novel, *Hope Leslie, or Early Times in the Massachusetts*, which also tells a story of captivity and interracial marriage, sympathetic to Native lives. Sedgwick's fiction confronted white Americans' views of Indians in the time period, appealing to "the enlightened and accurate observer of human nature," both writer and reader who might speak out about Indian removal policies in discussions that dominated 1820s America and that would lead by the next decade to the displacement of tens of thousands of American Indians from their indigenous lands.[13]

"The Catholic Iroquois," published in *The Atlantic Souvenir*, appeared in 1826, a year before *Hope Leslie*. In this earlier story, Sedgwick reverses the predominant captivity narrative of the period, to which her own family legends contributed. "The Catholic Iroquois" revises the genre, recalling the past as the future advances. It is the Old World giving way to the New, just as Sedgwick's grand tour and visit to Niagara Falls symbolized five years earlier.

From *Life and Letters of Catharine Maria Sedgwick* (1871)

1821

Buffalo, June 29th.—After we left Batavia the face of the country changed. It has quite a new look—here and there log houses, and fields full of stumps, but everywhere abundance and comfortable abodes.

This beautiful country stimulates my patriotism. That passion which is inspired by the peaceful triumphs of man over Nature, if it is not as romantic, is certainly more innocent than that which is kindled by battle-grounds, and I should even venture to put our cheerful dwellings, and fruitful fields, and blooming gardens against the ivy-mantled towers and blasted oaks of older regions, and busy hands and active minds against the 'spectres that sit and sigh' amid their ruins. You saw this place immediately after the devastation of the last war, during which every habitation save one was burnt. You would be surprised at its phoenix resurrection. There are 1200 inhabitants, three congregations, a beautiful Episcopal church, a bank, courthouse, and several fine brick houses, some of them quite as large as any in Albany. . . .

Niagara Falls, July 1st.—We arrived at the Falls yesterday at 1 o'clock, or, as they call the place here, at Stamford. We immediately obtained a guide, and all, with one heart and one mind, with the most impatient curiosity, descended to take our first view of the Falls. I know it is impossible to give an idea of the beauty and sublimity of the scene. If I fail to do it, I may impress my memory—so strongly as to be able at some future time to recall—the images that are before me at this moment. From Forsyth's the walk toward the Falls is for some distance through a level and shaded road; then you descend a deep pathway, with steep banks on each side, covered with a verdure that resembles the new-mown grass, fresh and sparkling from a recent shower—a beautiful peculiarity that it always preserves, and owes to the continual humidity of the atmosphere. These banks are overhung with butternut and beech trees, elms and lindens. Under a beautiful linden we first caught the view of the American Fall, which is directly in front of you as you approach the bank. This is one straight sheet of water, with a single interruption from a small intervening island, covered with evergreen. You see the rapids beyond it, the bridge Judge Porter has thrown over them to Goat Island, his fine house, almost hid by the majestic trees around it, and two little islands on the brink of the fall. They look, amidst the commotion, like the ships of some woodland nymph gayly sailing onward, or you might imagine the wish of the Persian girl realized, 'Oh, that this little isle had wings!' . . .

3d July. On board the steam-boat Ontario, Niagara River, Youngstown.—We left the Falls yesterday morning. The morning was rainy (the first rain we have had since we left home), but, notwithstanding, we all went through showers above and mud below to take our farewell of the Falls. Dear Robert, whose benevolence is indefatigable, was not willing to have me come away without going under Table Rock. We descended the steps once more together, and scrambled over the rocks, which in some places are so soft that you can break off pieces and crumble them to powder in your hands. We walked under the tremendous projection of rock, which here forms a considerable arc of a circle, the summit, as you stand in the depths of the excavations, projecting many yards beyond you, with trees hanging over the extreme point. Every thing is so vast that you seem introduced to a new state of being, and almost doubt your identity. The heights and the depths, the moisture of the atmosphere, which gives to every leaf and spear of grass in the crevices of the rocks a tender green; the fishermen below, who seem dwindled to children, all combine to form a scene as new as it is imposing. But it is not these banks of rock . . . , it is not that solitary and eternal torrent that produces the awe you feel, inspiring devotion amidst these objects, but it is the 'Spirit of God moving on the waters.' It is the vastness of every object, expressing the infinity of the Creator, and thus bringing you into his visible presence. . . .

We took our leave of the Falls with a mixture of sadness and gratitude. 'Glory had been at one entrance quite let in,' new images of the power and the glory of the Creator had been conveyed to our minds through this avenue, and our hearts united in a Te Deum for all that we had enjoyed from this marvelous work.

David Cusick: Appearing in Print

(c. 1780–c. 1840)

Print culture accompanied the rise of tourism to Niagara Falls, and the Tuscarora Indian Village was often included in travel guides to the Falls as a place to visit. The writer David Cusick (Tuscarora) would use print culture to great effect, shaping traveler's narratives to echo his own words and history.

When the editor of the *New Hampshire Patriot*, Isaac Hill, arrived at David Cusick's comfortable log home, in the Tuscarora Village in August 1826, he found Cusick perched on a bed "fantastically decorated with curtains," and "reading a newspaper." Newspaper publication had swelled to well over 500 by the mid-1820s, and local villages typically printed their own news, along with other pamphlets and almanacs. Print was a medium Cusick would use to great effect, not only in his book, *Sketches of Ancient History of the Six Nations* (1827), printed at the nearby Lewiston, New

York press, but also in travel narratives by others, like Hill's, where Cusick's character, voice, and Native history, came to life.

Access to print culture in the 1820s was significant for Cusick and other indigenous writers as a medium of resistance to land speculation and the violation of treaties. As one scholar puts it, "The struggle over treaty rights motivated the emergence of the first significant body of Native writing in English in the first half of the nineteenth century."[14] Cusick had applied for copyright in New York State for his *Sketches of Ancient History of the Six Nations* in January 1826. Though the first work authored in English by a Native writer in America was published in the early 1770s, Cusick's was the "first Native-authored, Native printed, and Native copyrighted text."[15] Later that year, around the time of Hill's visit in August 1826, in the region between present-day Tonawanda and Buffalo, New York, the Ogden Land Company circumvented treaty laws through fraud, bribery, and intimidation to purchase land from the Senecas at the Buffalo Creek Reservation. Renowned Seneca orator and diplomat Red Jacket traveled to the US capital to urge the Senate to reject the treaty's ratification. Though the Senate did not ratify the treaty, neither did it disapprove of it. The publication of David Cusick's history is timely: his voice was on the front lines of a broader movement to protest the taking of Native lands.

Though Cusick was born in Oneida territory and was educated at the missionary-run Hamilton Oneida Academy (now Hamilton College), his family relocated sometime around 1800 to join other Tuscarora living along the Niagara River. The Tuscarora relocated there after forced migration from North Carolina in the late eighteenth century, having been invited to join the now Six Nations (Haudenosaunee, or Iroquois) of his book's title. Cusick's father, Col. Nicholas Cusick, had served on the side of American colonists during the Revolutionary War and acted as a guard and interpreter for the French general Marquis de Lafayette.[16] Following in his father's footsteps, David Cusick served heroically as a guard along the Niagara River during the War of 1812. Though his postwar years are not well documented, by early 1820, Cusick begins appearing in travel narratives to the region. He is described as a doctor who was himself in somewhat poor health with "rheumatism." And, he is praised as a writer, artist, and historian.

Mention of Cusick's writing and paintings appear in other 1826 travel narratives, including that by Thomas L. McKenney, the first superintendent of what became the Bureau of Indian Affairs. The similarity of McKenney's travel book to Isaac Hill's narrative of meeting Cusick printed in the *New Hampshire Patriot*, as well as to others in the period, is striking. Each of the travelers who visited Cusick end up telling the same story: the curtained bed, the rheumatism, and the heroic Nicholas Cusick. They write of the Tuscarora migration and invitation to join the Five Nations (Mohawk, Oneida, Onondaga, Cayuga, and Seneca), forming the Six Nations. What is more, the visitors describe images and myths of the Six Nations based on paintings they saw in David Cusick's home, which they sometimes bought. Cusick may have intended to sell his *Sketches of Ancient History* to Niagara Falls tourists as well. The visitor's narratives detail conversations they had with Cusick, including the separation of nations by international borders; the taking of Seneca lands; and the remaining acreage of regional reservations. Though each writer closes his memories of Cusick with a reflection on the stereotype of the "disappearing Indian," Cusick's voice is everywhere present in the stories they tell. It might be said that he put words in the mouths of white authors. At the very least, Cusick was selling his history, both literally and figuratively, to tourists.

Cusick's *Sketches of Ancient History of the Six Nations* was popular over the next few decades. Short articles on it appeared in newspapers from Boston to Washington, DC, from Maine to Ohio to North Carolina. Cusick is acknowledged by one reviewer as having "placed himself at once among the *literati* of our country . . . and given a most interesting narrative to the public."[17] The *Atlantic Journal, and Friend of Knowledge* advertised Cusick's book in 1833, writing: "Very curious little work by a Tuscarora Indian, giving the traditions of the Onguy [Iroquois] tribes. The whole new and important for American history."[18]

Cusick's *Sketches* was indeed a "new and important" work for American history. It was part preservation of the historical traditions of the Six Nations, part performance of those traditions in the present, and part an authoritative claim to the land and its history. Cusick's work called into question European and American historical narratives of the "New World." He locates the time of the Six Nations well before—as well as after—the arrival of Europeans. Cusick writes, for instance, that 800 years before Columbus, land along the Niagara River was ceded from another indigenous nation to those of the Five Nations. And it was land subsequently defended against outside nations. Cusick's history thus challenges the story of "discovery" that settlers used to claim indigenous lands.

From *Sketches of Ancient History of the Six Nations*
(2nd edition, 1828)

In the reign the King Atotarho VIII, perhaps 450 years before Columbus discovered the America. About this time the Twakanhah or Messissaugers began to wage a war against the five nations ; the Senecas on the frontier were most engaged in the warfare. After various skirmishes the enemy was so excited that they determined to destroy the fort Kauhanauka, (now in Tuscarora near Lewiston,) but the commander of the fort was aware of the danger, he sent messengers to the forts in the vicinity, and about eight hundred warriors were collected at fort Kauhanauka. The commander had sent runners to observe the movements of the enemy. The army marched towards the river, and hid themselves among the bushes under the mountain ; the enemy came up ; a bloody battle ensued ; the enemy was repulsed and flies from the foe. The army retired to the fort ; soon after the commander dispatched two runners to the forts on the Genesee river to procure assistance as soon as possible ; the army received reinforcements ; they made bark canoes and carried them to the mouth of the Niagara river ; the canoes were ready, the commander sent a chieftain and offered the enemy an intermission of parley, but the proposal was not accepted ; the army immediately crossed the river and made vigorous attack : the enemy was routed and fled from the bank without making resistance, retreated towards the head of the lake ; after burning the huts, the army returned to the fort : but the commotions were not quelled ; small parties of the Senecas often take the canoes and go by water towards the head of Ontario lake, in search of the enemy, but they avoid from attack of superior force ; several engagements were made on the lake with small parties of the enemy ; after a while the commander of the fort Kauhanauka, was ardent to attack the main body of the enemy ; he sends runners beyond the Genesee river, and obtained two thousand warriors : the army again crossed the Niagara river and proceeded towards the head of the lake, but before reached the beach met a strong force of the enemy ; after a desperate contest the army retreated ;

the commander soon perceived that it was impossible to gain the conquest, sued for peace and offered to restore the prisoners which he took from them which was concluded.

Margaret Fuller: Sublime Satire

(1810–1850)

Four months after her visit to Niagara Falls in 1843, Margaret Fuller became the first woman given access to the Harvard Library Reading Room, a traditionally all-male institution. There, she researched material to write "Niagara," the first essay of her travel book, Summer on the Lakes, in 1843, *crafting in its pages a critique of male authority over the landscape.*

In a letter to Ralph Waldo Emerson after she left Niagara Falls, New York, Margaret Fuller remarks that her stay ended at the right time, before she lost reverence for the sublimity of the site. "I got so familiar," writes Fuller, "that I might have been tempted to address even the British fall with the easy impertinence of the Yankee visitor 'I wonder how many years you've been aroaring at this rate, I wonder if all you've been pouring could be ciphered on a slate.'"[19] Fuller takes these lines from a popular lyric of the Falls, which a tourist had inscribed in the pages of the *Table Rock Album*.[20] Whether Fuller read the words there or later, in the pages of a periodical at Harvard, is not clear. What is clear is her tone—she's poking a bit of fun at what's been said of the Falls.

With friends, Fuller had crossed New York State by train—a woman traveling alone would have been considered indecent. She had been given a parasol at the station just before departing New England. Little could her friend have predicted that it would serve to shield Fuller from snowflakes rather than an early summer rain or the sun's rays.[21] It seems hard to believe, even by Western New York standards, that snow fell from Rochester, New York to Cleveland, Ohio on June 1, 1843, just twenty days before the summer equinox.[22] The snowstorm blanketed the region three days after Fuller checked into room 38 of the prominent Cataract House Hotel[23] on the American side of the Falls. (See figure 4.) In another letter to Emerson she remarked: "We have had bad weather here, bitterly cold."[24]

Fuller stayed a week at the Falls, from May 28 to June 4, before her tour of what was then the Western Frontier: Michigan, Illinois, and Wisconsin, crossing by steamboat the Great Lakes Erie, Huron, and Michigan. Only days prior to her own journey westward from New England, nearly a thousand Americans would embark from Independence, Missouri, emigrating west on "the Oregon Trail," a journey preceded just five years earlier by the forced migration of tens of thousands of Native Americans from their Southeastern homelands on what came to be known as The Trail of Tears. Fuller was critical of American opportunists bent on westward expansion. During her stay at Niagara, she may have seen advertisements in newspapers such as the *Buffalo Courier* for "Sale of Indian Lands" in the Western New York region. She wrote of the displaced and oppressed, including Native Americans and frontier women, in an account of her travels, *Summer on the Lakes, in 1843*.[25]

Throughout her writing, Fuller's critical eye is as powerful as the Falls of Niagara. *Summer on the Lakes* appeared between her two very popular essays about the position of women in nineteenth-century Amer-

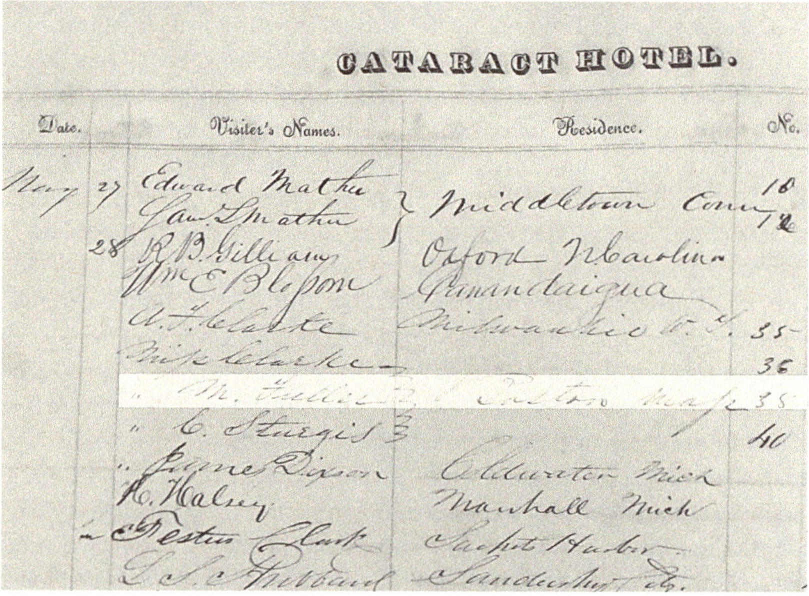

Figure 4. Margaret Fuller's Cataract House Hotel registration, May 28, 1843. Local History Library, Niagara Falls Public Library. Cataract House register, September 19, 1840 to April 30, 1844. Niagara Falls Public Library.

ica: "The Great Lawsuit: Man versus Men. Woman versus Women" (1843), and the longer meditation it evolved into, *Woman in the Nineteenth Century* (1845). In the opening essay to *Summer on the Lakes*, "Niagara," Fuller's views of the landscape are full of wit tempered only by her respect for nature. Here, her critique of human folly is aimed largely at male domination of the land.

Fuller was particularly annoyed with those who used the natural environment for their own self-interest, such as the tourist who disrupts her as she sits on Table Rock. Here, for a brief moment, she encounters the sublime: "There all power of observing details, all separate consciousness, was quite lost," she notes. Until, that is, a male tourist uses the location as a spittoon.

This utility, as Fuller names it, hardly surprises her. Gone were the days of nature as something to be feared and thus revered. By the early nineteenth century, nature had been "tamed" and "manufactured" by the development of towns, mills, canals, railroads, and landscape design. But what was now sought, ironically, was an escape from civilization—a romanticized notion of nature, with all of its rough and rustic elements, even if equally manufactured. To satirize this utilitarian approach to nature, Fuller cites the German Prince Hermann von Pückler-Muskau (1785–1871). Muskau was a writer and landscape gardener who had convinced the townspeople of Muskau, Germany[26] to sell him portions of their land so he could turn his family's estate into a vast park. He then fashioned it into a so-called rustic landscape, carving streams and sculpting hills. He installed a hermitage and hired "as its inhabitant a bearded old guardsman" to complete the scene.[27]

Fuller not only poked fun at aristocratic men abroad but also at the new money at home, including Niagara Falls local, General Peter B. Porter. Fuller, like Sedgwick, acknowledges Porter had "heroically planted the bridges by which we cross to Goat Island," even if it had to be rebuilt three times because nature kept destroying it.[28] Fuller satirizes Porter's achievement through allusions to Jack Downing and "Jonathan, our national hero," both popular stock characters in early American literature. The "Jonathan" figure, or "Brother Jonathan," as he was often called, notably made his first appearance in the genre of the political cartoon in 1776, and, in subsequent decades, became a humorous stereotype of the common American, the "everyman" of the new democracy. Jonathan was often portrayed as foolish, though not for long as his "take charge" or "self-reliant" attitude exemplified his American spirit of independence and individualism.[29] He was, like Jack Downing, a descendant of Yankee Doodle and a forerunner to Uncle Sam.[30]

Perhaps Fuller harnessed the Jonathan allusion to critique the Porters' ambition and domination. Her inclusion of these figures certainly lends a particularly American experience to her visit—as "familiar" as Jonathan, and "suitable" for Downing. What is this uniquely American experience though? Fuller follows her mention of Porter, Downing, and Jonathan with a serious commentary on warfare and humanity, which even a "temple" like Niagara Falls cannot change. She soon turns to an image of a chained eagle, that traditional symbol of American freedom, here rendered cruel and ironic, and which she likely saw at the Old Curiosity Shop, located behind the Cataract House Hotel. Fuller may have read Theodore G. Hulett's 1842 guidebook, *Every Man His Own Guide to the Falls of Niagara: Or the Whole Story in a Few Words*, which recounts "The Bald Eagle's Protest" by recalling battles fought at the Falls as the eagle flew free. The poem and the chained eagle were both showcased at Hulett's store.[31] To Fuller, the eagle's nobility far surpasses those who debase it.

Surrounded by so many instances of domination over the land, Fuller's approach to the landscape is all the more notable. She does—*nothing*. She simply walks and observes. Even the cold and the snow are not to be altered, let alone the Falls. Fuller's approach, different to her male contemporaries, is to be *present* in nature, rather than thinking of its utility: "I, like others, have little to say where the spectacle is, for once, great enough to fill the whole life, and supersede thought, giving us only its own presence. 'It is good to be here,' is the best as the simplest expression that occurs to the mind."

From "Niagara," *Summer on the Lakes, in 1843* (1844),
published under S. M. Fuller

Chapter I

Niagara, June 10, 1843.

. . .

As picture, the Falls can only be seen from the British side. There they are seen in their veils, and at sufficient distance to appreciate the magical effects of these, and the light and shade. From the boat, as you cross, the effects and contrasts are more melodramatic. On the road back from the whirlpool, we saw them as a reduced picture with delight. But what I liked best was to sit on Table Rock, close to the great fall. There all power of observing details, all separate consciousness, was quite lost.

Once, just as I had seated myself there, a man came to take his first look. He walked close up to the fall, and, after looking at it a moment, with an air as if thinking how he could best appropriate it to his own use, he spat into it.

This trait seemed wholly worthy of an age whose love of *utility* is such that the Prince Pückler-Muskau suggests the probability of men coming to put the bodies of their dead parents in the fields to fertilize them, and of a country such as Dickens has described; but these will not, I hope, be seen on the historic page to be truly the age or truly the America. A little leaven is leavening the whole mass for other bread.

The whirlpool I like very much. It is seen to advantage after the great falls; it is so sternly solemn. The river cannot look more imperturbable, almost sullen in its marble green, than it does just below the great fall; but the slight circles that mark the hidden vortex, seem to whisper mysteries the thundering voice above could not proclaim,—a meaning as untold as ever.

It is fearful, too, to know, as you look, that whatever has been swallowed by the cataract, is like to rise suddenly to light here, whether up-rooted tree, or body of man or bird. . . .

People complain of the buildings at Niagara, and fear to see it further deformed. I cannot sympathize with such an apprehension: the spectacle is capable to swallow up all such objects; they are not seen in the great whole, more than an earthworm in a wide field.

The beautiful wood on Goat Island is full of flowers; many of the fairest love to do homage here. The Wake Robin and May Apple are in bloom now; the former, white, pink, green, purple, copying the rainbow of the fall, and fit to make a garland for its presiding deity when he walks the land, for they are of imperial size, and shaped like stones for a diadem. Of the May Apple, I did not raise one green tent without finding a flower beneath.

And now farewell, Niagara. I have seen thee, and I think all who come here must in some sort see thee; thou art not to be got rid of as easily as the stars. I will be here again beneath some flooding July moon and sun. Owing to the absence of light, I have seen the rainbow only two or three times by day; the lunar bow not at all. However, the imperial presence needs not its crown, though illustrated by it.

General Porter and Jack Downing were not unsuitable figures here. The former heroically planted the bridges by which we cross to Goat Island, and the Wake-Robin-crowned genius has punished his temerity with deafness, which must, I think, have come upon him when he sank the first stone in the rapids. Jack seemed an acute and entertaining representative of Jonathan, come to look at his great water-privilege. He told us all about the Americanisms of the spectacle; that is to say, the battles that have been fought here. It seems strange that men could fight in such a place; but no temple can still the personal griefs and strifes in the breasts of its visitors.

No less strange is the fact that, in this neighborhood, an eagle should be chained for a plaything. When a child, I used often to stand at a window from which I could see an eagle chained in the balcony of a museum. The people used to poke at it with sticks, and my childish heart would swell with indignation as I saw their insults, and the mien with which they were borne by the monarch-bird. Its eye was dull, and its plumage soiled and shabby, yet, in its form and attitude, all the king was visible, though sorrowful and dethroned. . . .

Now, again, I saw him a captive, and addressed by the vulgar with the language they seem to find most appropriate to such occasions—that of thrusts and blows. Silently, his head averted, he ignored their existence, as Plotinus or Sophocles might that of a modern reviewer. Probably, he listened to the voice of the cataract, and felt that congenial powers flowed free, and was consoled, though his own wing was broken.

The story of the Recluse of Niagara[32] interested me a little. It is wonderful that men do not oftener attach their lives to localities of great beauty—that, when once deeply penetrated, they will let themselves so easily be borne away by the general stream of things, to live any where and any how. But there is something ludicrous in being the hermit of a show-place, unlike St. Francis in his mountain-bed, where none but the stars and rising sun ever saw him.

There is also a "guide to the falls," who wears his title labeled on his hat; otherwise, indeed, one might as soon think of asking for a gentleman usher to point out the moon. Yet why should we wonder at such, either, when we have Commentaries on Shakespeare, and Harmonics of the Gospels?

. . .

At last, slowly and thoughtfully I walked down to the bridge leading to Goat Island, and when I stood upon this frail support, and saw a quarter of a mile of tumbling, rushing rapids, and heard their everlasting roar, my emotions overpowered me, a choking sensation rose to my throat, a thrill rushed through my veins, "my blood ran rippling to my finger's ends." This was the climax of the effect which the falls produced upon me—neither the American nor the British fall moved me as did these rapids. For the magnificence, the sublimity of the latter I was prepared by descriptions and by paintings. When I arrived in sight of them I merely felt, "ah, yes, here is the fall, just as I have seen it in picture." When I arrived at the terrapin bridge, I expected to be overwhelmed, to retire trembling from this giddy eminence, and gaze with unlimited wonder and awe upon the immense mass rolling on and on, but, somehow or other, I thought only of comparing the effect on my mind with what I had read and heard. I looked for a short time, and then with almost a feeling of disappointment, turned to go to the other points of view to see if I was not mistaken in not feeling any surpassing emotion at this sight. But from the foot of Biddle's stairs, and the middle of the river, and from below the table rock, it was still "barren, barren all." And, provoked with my stupidity in feeling most moved in the wrong place, I turned away to the hotel, determined to set off for Buffalo that afternoon. But the stage did not go, and, after nightfall, as there was a splendid moon, I went down to the bridge, and leaned over the parapet, where the boiling rapids came down in their might. It was grand, and it was also gorgeous; the yellow rays of the moon made the broken waves appear like auburn tresses twining around the black rocks. But they did not inspire me as before. I felt a foreboding of a mightier emotion to rise up and swallow all others, and I passed on to the terrapin bridge. Everything was changed, the misty apparition had taken off its many-colored crown which it had worn by day, and a bow of silvery white spanned its summit. The moonlight gave a poetical indefiniteness to the distant parts of the waters, and while the rapids were glancing in her beams, the river below the falls was black as night, save where the reflection of the sky gave it the appearance of a shield of blued steel. No gaping tourists loitered, eyeing with their glasses, or sketching on cards the hoary locks of the ancient river god. All tended to harmonize with the natural grandeur of the scene. I gazed long. I saw how here mutability and unchangeableness were united. I surveyed the conspiring waters rushing against the rocky ledge to overthrow it at one mad plunge, till, like toppling ambition, o'erleaping themselves, they fall on t'other side, expanding into foam ere they reach the deep channel where they creep submissively away.

Then arose in my breast a genuine admiration, and a humble adoration of the Being who was the architect of this and of all. Happy were the first discoverers of Niagara, those who could come unawares upon this view and upon that, whose feelings were entirely their own. With what gusto does Father Hennepin describe "this great downfall of water," "this vast and prodigious cadence of water, which falls down after a surprising and astonishing manner, insomuch that the universe does not afford its parallel. 'Tis true Italy and Swedeland boast of some such things, but we may well say that they be sorry patterns when compared with this of which we do now speak."

Chapter 2

Clean Water and Clean Air

The rise of tourism to Niagara Falls was connected to the human relationship to nature—both aesthetic and medicinal. As European tastes continued to be transported to the New World, views of the landscape changed. Once viewed as a wilderness in need of control, nature was now sought as an escape from civilization. By the early nineteenth century, tourists set out in search of panoramas of "unspoiled" nature. But it was not enough simply to observe the landscape. The search for "the picturesque"—natural settings that were pleasing to the eye—gave way to discussions of beauty and the effect of the landscape on the senses. Travel to such places as the Falls, with its geographic greatness, could create a feeling of connection with all of nature and the infinite, or divine.

In poetry, essays, and travel narratives, writers and tourists expressed belief in the transformative power of nature on the mind and senses. But there were physical benefits, too. By 1830, guidebooks to Niagara Falls advertised mineral springs that offered healing for many types of ailments. The Bellevue mineral spring, for example, located two miles from the Falls toward the Whirlpool Rapids, was advertised to have "sulphuretted hydrogen and carbonic acid gasses" that had "curative properties." Its waters could supposedly benefit rheumatism, gout, "congestions of the blood," "slow fever," "depression of the stomach," indigestion, "flatulent cholic," "worms," "leprous sores," and "several diseases peculiar to females," among other complaints.[1] Though the list might sound excessive today, natural springs and the "spas" that eventually built up around them drew on the belief, dating to antiquity, in the therapeutic value of mineral water.

It was not until the mid-nineteenth century, during the second outbreak of cholera in the early 1850s, after Washington Irving's visit to the Falls, that clean water was understood as crucial to public health. For Henry David Thoreau, it was the curative climate of the Falls, what Catherine Maria Sedgwick noted as the "continual humidity of the atmosphere," that beckoned. Others, such as Henry Wadsworth Longfellow, were drawn to the Falls for the mental health benefits of immersion in nature that are valued again today.[2]

Washington Irving: The Canal and Cholera

(1783–1859)

With the outbreak of the cholera epidemic in the summer of 1832, Washington Irving was fortunate to evade illness on his way to Niagara Falls. His second visit to the Falls in 1853, however, was plagued by "a violent fever and delirium."[3]

After seventeen years in Europe, and forty days at sea, Washington Irving was eager to return home in May 1832 to see how the American landscape had changed during his long absence. Behind him, cholera continued its yearlong ravage, first in England and then France, from where he sailed. Little could Irving have known that shortly after his arrival in New York another ship crossing the Atlantic bound for Quebec carried the illness.

Irving set out on his American tour on July 9, 1832. Aboard a private barge heading up the Hudson River to West Point and then the Catskills, he writes to his brother Peter of seeing "the veritable haunts of Rip Van Winkle," his well-known character from *The Sketch Book of Geoffrey Crayon, Gent.* (1819).[4] Life seemed to be imitating art. Rip van Winkle had famously slept through the American Revolution and woke to a changed world. Irving was waking to the marvels of modern travel, the joys of picturesque American sites, and the good companionship of like-minded "ramblers."[5]

The tour took Irving first to Boston and the White Mountains of New Hampshire. After a brief return to the city and a visit with family at Tarrytown, New York, he journeyed again up the Hudson River to Albany, Schenectady, and Saratoga Springs, then across the state to Niagara Falls, Lake Erie, and on to the Western prairies.[6] A century earlier, getting to

Niagara Falls was arduous. Over the course of the eighteenth century, footpaths were slowly widened for carriages, and inns were established to house the weary traveler.[7] By the early nineteenth century, the Niagara frontier region was accessible via the Erie Canal on the US side in 1825, and Canada's Welland Canal in 1829. But new access also brought new dangers.

Throughout the summer and fall of 1832 more ships that had unknowingly transported cholera were docking in the New York Harbor. The disease had begun to travel the waterways of Lower Canada and New York State as well as regions west and south. The first case of cholera recorded in North America was reported in Quebec on June 8. Outbreaks were recorded along the St. Lawrence by mid-June, reportedly reaching Niagara Falls, New York as early as June 22.[8] Quarantines were imposed at the New York harbor and along the Erie Canal. Wealthy families evacuated cities, particularly New York City, wishing to remove themselves from the "corrupted atmosphere" they mistakenly associated with the city's poor, immigrant working classes. In the era before cholera was understood to be an infectious disease, the upper classes failed to realize that lack of access in these communities to uncontaminated drinking water was vital. Cholera, however, did not discriminate.

With good fortune and the leisure of the writer-tourist, Irving happened to get out of New York at the right time. In the first days of his voyage, he makes little mention of the illness, dismissing general concern. He writes to the just-returned ambassador to London and soon-to-be vice president–elect, Martin van Buren, that, "New York is almost deserted through the exaggerated alarm concerning the cholera, which is not more to be dreaded by decent people here than it was in London." Irving shares the class-based view of the period that those subject to the fatal illness do not include the gentry.

Nevertheless, his letters written from across the state provide a glimpse into the atmosphere of that summer and of Irving's own increasing concern over "the malady." In letters and journals written from Saratoga Springs and New York City, he laments the unavailability of "pure water" in the city, and is "quite grieved that the cholera and other 'various causes'" prevent him from meeting a friend "on the banks of the Hudson." He notes in his journal: "Albany half deserted on a/c of the cholera."[9] He determines by mid-August to bypass Utica "though hitherto I have never avoided the malady, nor shall I do so in the course of my tour."[10] Irving and company in fact avoided the Erie Canal altogether, traveling instead by stagecoach across New York state.

The choice is notable. Irving set out on tour to discover a "new" America. The Erie Canal, still in its early years, was itself a sight to be seen.[11] And though by the 1830s, stage coach design had improved with better suspension to lessen a bumpy ride, coach travel was still uncomfortable and a slower way to go. Roads were in the process of being widened and leveled, but mudholes and log "corduroy roads" over marshy regions remained. Irving chose the slower, arguably less comfortable route. Perhaps he was more concerned about exposure to cholera than he let on.

Niagara Falls proved worth the journey, however. By Thursday, August 23, 1832, Irving passed through "Lewistown," present-day Lewiston, New York, where he and his companions likely boarded one of two four-horse coach lines, the Barton or the Pioneer, before continuing on to Niagara Falls by sunset.[12] The group stayed on the American side of the Falls but toured "the English side" as well, crossing the river three times, the last including a drive to Brock's Monument, the memorial to General Isaac Brock who defeated an American invasion in the War of 1812 at Queenston Heights. Irving's visit lasted just two full days, with a 5:00 a.m. departure to Buffalo on Sunday, August 26, but it was enough time for him to compose a detailed "sketch" of the Falls, both visual and written. It was a landscape that clearly mesmerized him, both the natural landscape, and the one built during his years abroad. And, he had avoided cholera.

Irving found the Falls less mesmerizing on his second visit in mid-August 1853, however, when illness would finally catch up with him. He writes to his friend, John Pendleton Kennedy, whom he had first met in 1832, that his doctor recommended a break from his intensive work on the biography of his namesake, George Washington. Irving's nephew Pierre Irving quotes his uncle saying, "I believe all that I require is a good spell of *literary abstinence*."

On the first of August, Irving met Kennedy in Saratoga Springs whose waters promised good health. Just over a week later, fatigued with tourists, the pair moved on to a nostalgic trip to Ogdensburg, New York, which Irving had visited fifty years prior. Next stop was Niagara Falls. After crossing Lake Ontario, Irving traveled again by carriage from "Lewistown," and then spent "an insufferably hot day" at the Falls. The heat "deranged his whole system," he writes.

Upon his return home, he was "taken down with a violent fever and delirium," followed by several days of upset stomach. He finds he must apologize to his traveling companion Kennedy, whose "bantering at Niagara" found Irving "a little techy," "too miserably out of tune to be played upon." The "malady" hung on for several days,[13] and when Kennedy visited him at the end of the month, noted in his journal: "Irving is just recovering from a severe attack of fever which has greatly reduced him since we parted at Niagara."[14]

Fortunately, Irving's health held out on that earlier visit in 1832. His journal entries from then captured his immediate impressions of the landscape, both written and drawn sketches recorded in the moment of first views not to be forgotten.[15] (See figure 5.) Enjoying a rest on Goat Island at the American Falls, Irving notes: "place for Summer nap." Reminiscent of Rip van Winkle, Irving might be said to weave his visit to the Falls into the tapestry of his early American literary legends.

From *American Journals* (1832)[16]

Friday, August 24

Beautiful view of Falls on Cloudy morng. at first the prospect in cloud[?] colouring then a break of Sunshine lighting up opposite side & gradually passing athwart the whole abyss—descend to the foot of the falls—

Afternoon cross to the English side—Great yawning Hotels overlooking the falls.

Swallows playing about in the mist of the falls

Saturday, August 25

1/2 past 9 oclock morng. on the stage over the falls, beautiful transparency of the water bright . . . feathery look of water—mist . . . all illuminated—rainbow forming a halo. The whole wonderfully brilliant & light—drops like chrystal chandolier . . . —foam below[?] like snow

12 oclock. By the cabin beside the American Fall. . . . Seated on a stone in fine grove of oaks & maples—Spray of . . . water

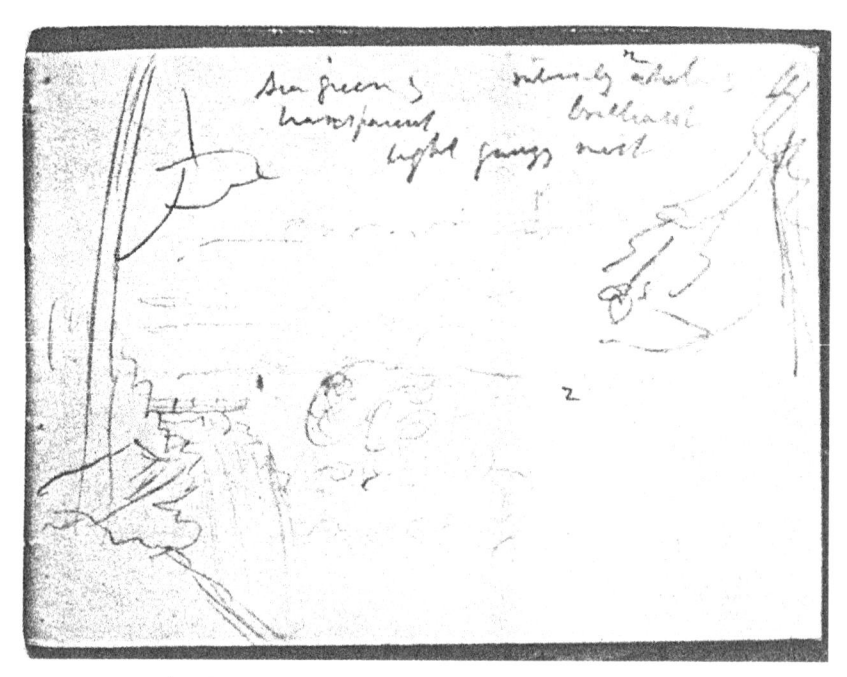

Figure 5. Sketch reproduced from *Washington Irving: Journals and Notebooks*, vol. 5, *1832–1859*, ed. Sue Fields Ross, pp. 30–31. Twayne Author's Series. Date of entries in Irving's journal: August 31, 1832.

falling on me—. . . View on the Am. fall to the Horseshoe looks like one constant fall[?]—lulling sound of water—Cool breeze from the falls—place for Summer nap.

Henry David Thoreau: Breath and Botany

(1817–1862)

In the spring of 1861, Henry David Thoreau's doctor prescribed travel to a healthier climate to treat his tuberculosis. Thoreau opted for the natural bounty of the West. Niagara Falls was to be his "first stop of consequence"—a place where he could study nature, even if the climate proved unhelpful.

Long before his visit to Niagara Falls in 1861, the American essayist Henry David Thoreau well knew that the pursuit of understanding nature was "the marrow of life," as his celebrated *Walden* (1854) put it. It was certainly more a vocation to him than any commercial endeavor.

In March 1842 he had visited "an old schoolmate who is going to help make the Welland Canal navigable for ships around Niagara." The Canal had been completed in 1829, but by 1842, an increase in larger ships necessitated an expanded canal, with fewer and longer locks. Thoreau notes in his journal that his former classmate, desiring to make a good living, "cannot see any such motives and modes of living as I. . . . And so we go silently different ways, with all serenity." The journal entry is an apt metaphor for two paths charted in nineteenth-century attitudes toward the landscape—the natural and the technological sublime. Where for some, nature was a place of "awe and reverence," for others, such emotional, psychological and aesthetic responses lay in "the technological conquest of matter."[17] Thoreau understood the value of industry and progress and the great interest in technological development. "Well and good," he concedes.[18] But it was not the life for him. That year he first used the Latin name of a plant in his journal.[19]

But though nature beckoned, it was ultimately illness that compelled Thoreau to journey west from New England in 1861. He had caught a cold in December 1860, causing him to develop flu-like symptoms and confining him to bed for several days.[20] The illness weakened him, and he could not shake a lingering cough that had turned into bronchitis. He lost weight and became housebound—"imprisoned," as this devotee of the natural world and walking excursions put it. In early May, 1861, he wrote to a friend:

> there is danger that the cold weather may come again, before I get over my bronchitis. The Doctor accordingly tells me that I must "clear out," to the West Indies, or elsewhere, he does not seem to care much where. But I decide against the West Indies, on account of their muggy heat in the summer, & the S. of Europe, on ac of the expense of time & money, and have at last concluded that it will be most expedient for me to try the air of Minnesota.

Thoreau determines that his "first stop of consequence" on this curative tour will be Niagara Falls. Nature was still foremost in his mind.

Notably traveling by train, Thoreau departed Concord, Massachusetts on May 11, 1861, stopping first in Worcester and then on to Albany, New York, where he and his traveling companion, the seventeen-year-old aspiring naturalist Horace Mann Jr., boarded the New York Central Railroad. Though Thoreau was skeptical of the train as a symbol of progress, it afforded a much faster journey than the Canal had to the previous generation.[21] Thoreau and Mann arrived at what was then Suspension Bridge Village[22] late in the evening on May 14, 1861, and began searching for a place to stay for the night. Their choices included the Monteagle "(a *high house*)," the Western House, and the New York Central Hotel, where they booked a room for $1.50. The following morning they traveled the two miles to Niagara Falls, first searching for a nearby boardinghouse for the week. There was little vacancy, but they finally found a room for $1 per day at the American House.[23] It had not yet been destroyed by fire as it was on Emerson's visit two years later.

By the afternoon, Thoreau, feeling in good health, was out walking on Goat Island, noting the variety of flora thriving in the humid vicinity of the Falls. He spent at least three of his afternoons observing nature: measuring trees, collecting and pressing specimens of plants and flowers, and identifying species. (See figures 6 and 7.) Most of the plants were in bloom, or at the end of their blooms, albeit surprisingly, since it had been a cold spring. Thoreau notes seeing ice under the cliffs as late as mid-May. The bracing air seems not to have had the effect on his health he had hoped, however, as his two purchases of throat lozenges suggest he was still unwell.[24]

Thoreau's complete journey west lasted two months. By the end of July, 1861, the *New York Tribune* would relate news of his poor health. He would never wholly recover, and on May 6, 1862, almost a full year after his visit to Niagara Falls, he died of tuberculosis. A bounty of evidence remains of his visit, however. He spent less time, it appears, in looking at the Falls and recording his impressions than he does in carefully observing its surrounding foliage—leaving behind a botanical time-capsule.

From Thoreau's 1861 Journals[25]

May 15

> To Niagara Falls. P.m. to Goat Island. Sight of rapids, from the Bridge like sea off Cape Cod,—most imposing sight as yet. The great apparent height of the waves tumbling over the immense ledges—at a distance; while the water view is broad & boundless in that direction as if you were looking out to sea, you are so low.

Yet the distances are very deceptive; the most distant billow was scarcely more than a quarter of a mile off, though it appeared two miles or more. Many ducks constantly floating a little way down the rapids, then flying back & alighting again. . . .

Masses of ice under edge of cliff.

The prevailing trees on Goat Island are the beech, bass, — the former most forward in leafing, —sugar-maple, arbor-vitae, red cedar, ostrya(?) elm, hemlock, and hornbeam. The most conspicuous flowers in bloom were the large white *trillium*, with leaves and sepals of very various width and form (*Trillium grandiflorum*); *Trillium erectum* (dark purple); much less common with us; both these in flower. The first whitens large tracks of woodland as seen from the railroad in New York State.

Also *Claytonia Virginica* (spring-beauty) is very common, forming large patches spotted with white(?) as does the *Dentaria laciniata*. The former, indeed both of them, are a little ahead of the white *trillium* in time. The *D. l.* varies from pale purple to white.

The *Dicentra cucullaria* perhaps is next most noticeable, with its very handsome low-spreading, finely-divided leaves, and its erect spike of whitish flowers. (April in flower.) The May-apple leaves are as large as ever, and it is strongly flower-budded, and stands in more or less dense patches, like little green umbrellas.

Dog's-tooth violet has just about *done*, but has been very common. *Aralia trifolia* well in flower; generally quite low and delicate.

Arabis lyrata leaves and white flowers. (April in flower.)
Perhaps *Orchis spectabilis* in bud.
Viola pubescens, (April in flower). *Viola pedata*.
Ranunculus abortivus in bloom.
Ribes cynosbati, with prickly fruit, in flower. (Yet stamens and pistils longer than calyx.) Very common.
Cohosh just in bloom.
Lepidium campestre in bloom and going to seed.
Cardamine (*rhomboidea*-like)?— purplish flowers.
Amelanchier, downy variety, thirty feet high, in full bloom, but leaves less open than *Botrychium* near, which is not quite out.
Shepherdia Canadensis. At north end of isle, ice under the cliff.

Figure 6. Henry David Thoreau Herbarium, Goat Island plant pressing, May 15, 1861. Image 21, Box 2, Portfolio 1, Folder 3: Specimen 2: *Dentaria diphylla*. M. Brown, Brattleboro. *Dentaria laciniata* [GH521017]. Courtesy Harvard University Herbaria.

Figure 7. Henry David Thoreau Herbarium, Goat Island plant pressing, May 15, 1861. Image 590; Box 26, Portfolio 6, Folder 3: Specimen 2: *T. erectum*. M. Brown, Brattleboro. *Trillium cernuum, Trillium grandiflorum*, Goat Island [GH01082446]. Courtesy Harvard University Herbaria.

Henry Wadsworth Longfellow: Mourning and Melancholy

(1807–1882)

Perhaps no writer visited Niagara Falls in greater despair than the poet Henry Wadsworth Longfellow. Even the majestic nature of the Falls could not long lift his spirit.

A year after the tragic death of his beloved wife, Fanny Appleton Longfellow, in 1861, which occurred just three months after the start of the American Civil War, the popular nineteenth-century poet Henry Wadsworth Longfellow set out on a needed restorative journey. It was to be his first time seeing Niagara Falls.

In the days, weeks, and months following the start of the Civil War on April 12, 1861, Longfellow's journal records great sadness. "It is indeed a heavy atmosphere to breathe," he writes on May 2: "—the impending doom of a nation."[26] This national crisis was soon outweighed by personal tragedy, however.

On July 9, 1861 the unimaginable happened. Using wax to seal a package in the library of their home, with her daughters around her, a fallen match or a candle set fire to Fanny's light summer dress. Unable to put out the rapidly consuming flames, she was severely burned. Longfellow wounded his hands and face trying to save her. She did not recover. Fanny Longfellow died on July 10, 1861, the start of a life of mourning for the poet.

On a rainy day in early June 1862, nearly a year after Fanny's tragic death, Longfellow set out for Niagara with his sons and with friends, including members of his wife's family. "On, on, on, all day long," he notes at the outset of this trip.[27] First Albany, then on to Utica on June 5, with a visit to Trenton Falls, New York. By June 7, the group arrived at Niagara where they stayed at the Cataract House Hotel, Longfellow in room 167. His first glimpse of the Falls was by moonlight.

The following day, a Sunday, Longfellow spent "all the morning alone, on Goat Island" and the Three Sisters Islands. The solitude in nature must have been good for his spirits, as he notes: "What a lovely spot! Better than a church for me to-day." Like many others before and after him, Longfellow found religious and spiritual meaning in the Falls.

He wrote a letter home that day to his younger daughters Edie and Annie indicating how much they likely wanted to attend this sabbatical, and how much he missed them. "I saw this morning a little girl, just as big as Annie holding her Papa's hand," he recounts,

> and walking on a light wooden bridge, over the Rapids. She wore a little red jacket, and looked so much like my own darling, that the tears came into my eyes, I wanted to see you so much. Dont [sic] you think she was too small to come to Niagara?[28]

Despite his own needs for his children's presence, Longfellow also desired to keep them safe. He assures his daughters he and his fellow travelers are all well and promises to purchase souvenirs when the shops reopen for the work week. (See figure 8.)

Though Longfellow's time at the Falls may have brought some respite from his grief, his joy is short-lived. By the third day of his visit,

Figure 8. Longfellow family and friends at Niagara Falls. Museum collection, LONG 5160. Courtesy of the National Park Service, Longfellow House, Washington's Headquarters, national historic site.

Clean Water and Clean Air / 39

he confesses that the Falls have not restored his calm but rather induced his unease:

> Niagara is too much for me; my nerves shake like a bridge of wire; a vague sense of terror and unrest haunts me all the time. My head swims and reels with the ceaseless motion of the water.

Longfellow took a farewell ramble that evening on Goat Island, Luna Island, and the Three Sisters Islands and then departed the next day for Toronto. Upon his return to Boston a week later, his despair is again palpable: "Bright, melancholy day. It is too terrible to bear! This utter loneliness!" On the first anniversary of Fanny's death, words fail him: "I can make no record of these days," he writes. "Better leave them wrapped in silence. Perhaps some day God will give me peace."[29]

From Life of Henry Wadsworth Longfellow,
June 1862

> 8th. A bright, beautiful day. Pass all the morning alone, on Goat Island and a smaller one, just on the western brink of the American Fall. What a lovely spot! Better than a church for me to-day. Go up the stone tower in the midst of the English Fall. It drives me frantic with excitement. In the afternoon, go over the suspension bridge to Table Rock, on the Canada side. It is the finest view of the English Fall. In every other particular the American side is preferable.

Chapter 3

The Falls and Fame

Early celebrity is sometimes followed by downfall or obscurity. As it is true today, so was it true in previous centuries. When the Irish poet Thomas Moore (1779–1852) arrived at the "British" side of the Falls on July 22, 1804, he was arguably a celebrity. His lyrical poetry had already made his name known at home and abroad, and he would soon establish friendships with the renowned British poet Lord Byron and the beloved American writer Washington Irving.

Like today's celebrities, Moore was given special treatment when he visited the Falls. In his letters home and in later reflections, he remarked on "a poor watchmaker at Niagara, who did a very necessary and difficult job" for him and refused payment, only too honored to have met the poet. Similarly, the captain of the ship Moore traveled on across Lake Ontario to Quebec also refused payment and offered to do the same for any of Moore's friends.[1]

A century later, however, Moore's star was eclipsed, if not at home in Ireland, then at least abroad. As a biographer notes in 1904, it was Moore's personality, his "compelling power," that made him a celebrity.[2] After his death, without his "presence," his work fell into obscurity. Nearly another century passed before Moore's fame was once again illuminated, this time earning him a historic marker in Niagara-on-the-Lake, Ontario, Canada.

Other writers, such as Sir Arthur Conan Doyle, already famous at the time of their visit, similarly used the Falls to their advantage. Not all writers were as fortunate as Moore and Conan Doyle, however. Some, relatively "unknown," such as Nathaniel Hawthorne, and seeking to establish a reputation, such as Oscar Wilde, hoped instead that the Falls might power their fame.

Nathaniel Hawthorne: Riding the Tide of Tourism

(1804–1864)

It must have been with great effort that Nathaniel Hawthorne departed Salem, Massachusetts, for a tour of New England, New York, and Quebec in September 1832; he had spent the handful of previous years in long periods of seclusion. But he was in pursuit of his destiny—to become a famous writer—and a writer needs a public.

If his trip had not been delayed by the cholera epidemic in the summer of 1832, Nathaniel Hawthorne may have crossed paths with Washington Irving on his journey to Niagara Falls, and his reputation may have gotten the jumpstart he was looking for. Though he began publishing short stories, or sketches and tales, as early as 1832, it was not until his 1837 *Twice-Told Tales* that he gained some recognition, with his most significant work, including *The Scarlet Letter* (1850) and *The House of the Seven Gables* (1851), not appearing until nearly two decades later.

With his mind set on a literary future in 1832, it is no wonder Hawthorne felt disappointment when the trip was deferred from June until September due to the outbreak of cholera in Lower Canada and much of New York State along the Erie Canal. As he wrote to his friend, the future President Franklin Pierce, he was, "very desirous of making this journey, on account of a book by which I intend to acquire an (undoubtedly) immense literary reputation."[3] Hawthorne thought this reputation could be staked on the fame of well-known American locales. A decade into the emerging tourism industry, the popularity of travel narratives and guidebooks likely seemed promising. Though not ultimately published in the form he had planned, his travel sketches illuminate the historical and technological developments of the period that helped to set him on his path to success.[4]

Hawthorne traveled to Niagara Falls on the Erie Canal, then in its seventh year. He had generally lived in seclusion in his family's home for the same amount of time. Now he was plunged into close confinement with other passengers. It was a slow journey, but the time afforded him development of his skills of observation. And his job of writer-observer afforded him a buffer from much interaction with others.

In his essay of the experience, "The Canal Boat," published in 1835, Hawthorne's journey takes place as much in his mind as on the water:

"The intolerable dullness of the scene engendered an evil spirit in me," he writes. He imagines that an Englishman on board, whom he sees writing in a corner, is caricaturizing the other passengers, including Hawthorne. It is, more likely, a projection of Hawthorne's own writerly creations, though the contest to establish an American literature against British literary prominence was a real one.[5] And travel narratives by British writers had provided particularly strong critiques of American mannerisms:

> Perceiving that the Englishman was taking notes in a memorandum-book, with occasional glances round the cabin, I presumed that we were all to figure in a future volume of travels, and amused my ill-humor by falling into the probable vein of his remarks. He would hold up an imaginary mirror, wherein our reflected faces would appear ugly and ridiculous, yet still retain an undeniable likeness to the originals. Then, with more sweeping malice, he would make these caricatures the representatives of great classes of my countrymen.

Seeing his companions now through the imagined lens of this foreign writer, Hawthorne similarly gives himself free reign to satirize American "types"—the school master, the farmer, the minister, the merchant, the lady. And in so doing, he satirizes himself most of all. Hawthorne was honing his skills as a travel writer. At Niagara Falls, he mastered the representative caricature of the tourist.

From his packet boat on the Canal, Hawthorne made his way to Lewiston, New York, most likely staying at the Frontier House,[6] before journeying on to "Manchester," an early name for the city of Niagara Falls. The city expressed hope of its own fame, its namesake the industrialized city in England. On September 27, 1832, Hawthorne checked in to the Cataract House Hotel and handed off his coat to a black waiter at what would become an important station on the Underground Railroad by the end of that decade.[7]

Ultimately, Hawthorne hesitated to see the Falls. He recognized that other well-known writers had already shaped his views. Instead, he observes the tourists he sees, turning them into types as he did in "The Canal Boat," and like those Arthur Lumley would later illustrate in *Niagara Seen with Different Eyes*. (See figure 1, Prologue.) Hawthorne caricaturizes adventurers and traders; the distracted mother and the uninterested child; the American unable to see the sites without a guide book; the artist who

The Falls and Fame / 43

would have better designed the Falls. The only tourist not made an object of Hawthorne's satire is the "pilgrim," like himself, complete with staff, dressed simply in "American homespun,"[8] a solitary figure in the landscape.

Despite his astute observations and early attempt at fame, Hawthorne's effort to pair his travel sketches with short stories in a larger volume he called "The Storyteller" had failed. The collection was rejected by publishers. He separated the pieces and published them individually, to lesser effect than he had hoped. When his Niagara essay did appear in 1835, it was in the monthly periodical *The New-England Magazine*, with a byline that identified him only as the author of another story, "The Gray Champion," something like a hypertext reference that directed the essay's reader to more of Hawthorne's work—but without actually naming him as author. The writer of "My Visit to Niagara" was anonymous. The travel essay ultimately did not bring him the fame he sought, but it offers a sketch of life at a moment when tourism to the Falls was on the rise.

From "My Visit to Niagara" (1835)

NEVER DID a pilgrim approach Niagara with deeper enthusiasm, than mine. I had lingered away from it, and wandered to other scenes, because my treasury of anticipated enjoyments, comprising all the wonders of the world, had nothing else so magnificent, and I was loath to exchange the pleasures of hope for those of memory so soon. At length, the day came. The stage-coach, with a Frenchman and myself on the back seat, had already left Lewiston, and in less than an hour would set us down in Manchester. I began to listen for the roar of the cataract, and trembled with a sensation like dread, as the moment drew nigh, when its voice of ages must roll, for the first time, on my ear. The French gentleman stretched himself from the window, and expressed loud admiration, while, by a sudden impulse, I threw myself back and closed my eyes. When the scene shut in, I was glad to think, that for me the whole burst of Niagara was yet in futurity. We rolled on, and entered the village of Manchester, bordering on the falls.

I am quite ashamed of myself here. Not that I ran, like a madman, to the falls, and plunged into the thickest of the spray—never stopping to breathe, till breathing was impossible: not that I committed this, or any other suitable extravagance.

On the contrary, I alighted with perfect decency and composure, gave my cloak to the black waiter, pointed out my baggage, and inquired, not the nearest way to the cataract, but about the dinner-hour. The interval was spent in arranging my dress. Within the last fifteen minutes, my mind had grown strangely benumbed, and my spirits apathetic, with a slight depression, not decided enough to be termed sadness. My enthusiasm was in a deathlike slumber. Without aspiring to immortality, as he did, I could have imitated that English traveler, who turned back from the point where he first heard the thunder of Niagara, after crossing the ocean to behold it. Many a western trader, by-the-by, has performed a similar act of heroism with more heroic simplicity, deeming it no such wonderful feat to dine at the hotel and resume his route to Buffalo or Lewiston, while the cataract was roaring unseen.

Such has often been my apathy, when objects, long sought, and earnestly desired, were placed within my reach. After dinner—at which, an unwonted and perverse epicurism detained me longer than usual—I lighted a cigar and paced the piazza, minutely attentive to the aspect and business of a very ordinary village. Finally, with reluctant step, and the feeling of an intruder, I walked towards Goat Island. At the toll-house, there were further excuses for delaying the inevitable moment. My signature was required in a huge leger, containing similar records innumerable, many of which I read. The skin of a great sturgeon, and other fishes, beasts, and reptiles; a collection of minerals, such as lie in heaps near the falls; some Indian moccasins, and other trifles, made of deer-skin and embroidered with beads; several newspapers from Montreal, New York, and Boston; all attracted me in turn. Out of a number of twisted sticks, the manufacture of a Tuscarora Indian, I selected one of curled maple, curiously convoluted, and adorned with the carved images of a snake and a fish. Using this as my pilgrim's staff, I crossed the bridge. Above and below me were the rapids, a river of impetuous snow, with here and there a dark rock amid its whiteness, resisting all the physical fury, as any cold spirit did the moral influences of the scene. On reaching Goat Island, which separates the two great segments of the falls, I chose the right-hand path, and followed it to the edge of the American cascade. There, while the falling sheet was yet invisible, I saw the vapor that never vanishes, and the Eternal Rainbow of Niagara. . . .

The last day that I was to spend at Niagara, before my departure for the far west, I sat upon the Table Rock. This celebrated station did not now, as of old, project fifty feet beyond the line of the precipice, but was shattered by the fall of an immense fragment, which lay distant on the shore below. Still, on the utmost verge of the rock, with my feet hanging over it, I felt as if suspended in the open air. Never before had my mind been in such perfect unison with the scene. There were intervals, when I was conscious of nothing but the great river, rolling calmly into the abyss, rather descending than precipitating itself, and acquiring tenfold majesty from its unhurried motion. It came like the march of Destiny. It was not taken by surprise, but seemed to have anticipated, in all its course through the broad lakes, that it must pour their collected waters down this height. The perfect foam of the river, after its descent, and the ever varying shapes of mist, rising up, to become clouds in the sky, would be the very picture of confusion, were it merely transient, like the rage of a tempest. But when the beholder has stood awhile, and perceives no lull in the storm, and considers that the vapor and the foam are as everlasting as the rocks which produce them, all this turmoil assumes a sort of calmness. It soothes, while it awes the mind.

Leaning over the cliff, I saw the guide conducting two adventurers behind the falls. It was pleasant, from that high seat in the sunshine, to observe them struggling against the eternal storm of the lower regions, with heads bent down, now faltering, now pressing forward, and finally swallowed up in their victory. After their disappearance, a blast rushed out with an old hat, which it had swept from one of their heads. The rock, to which they were directing their unseen course, is marked, at a fearful distance on the exterior of the sheet, by a jet of foam. The attempt to reach it, appears both poetical and perilous, to a looker-on, but may be accomplished without much more difficulty or hazard, than in stemming a violent northeaster. In a few moments, forth came the children of the mist. Dripping and breathless, they crept along the base of the cliff, ascended to the guide's cottage, and received, I presume, a certificate of their achievement, with three verses of sublime poetry on the back. (See figure 9.)

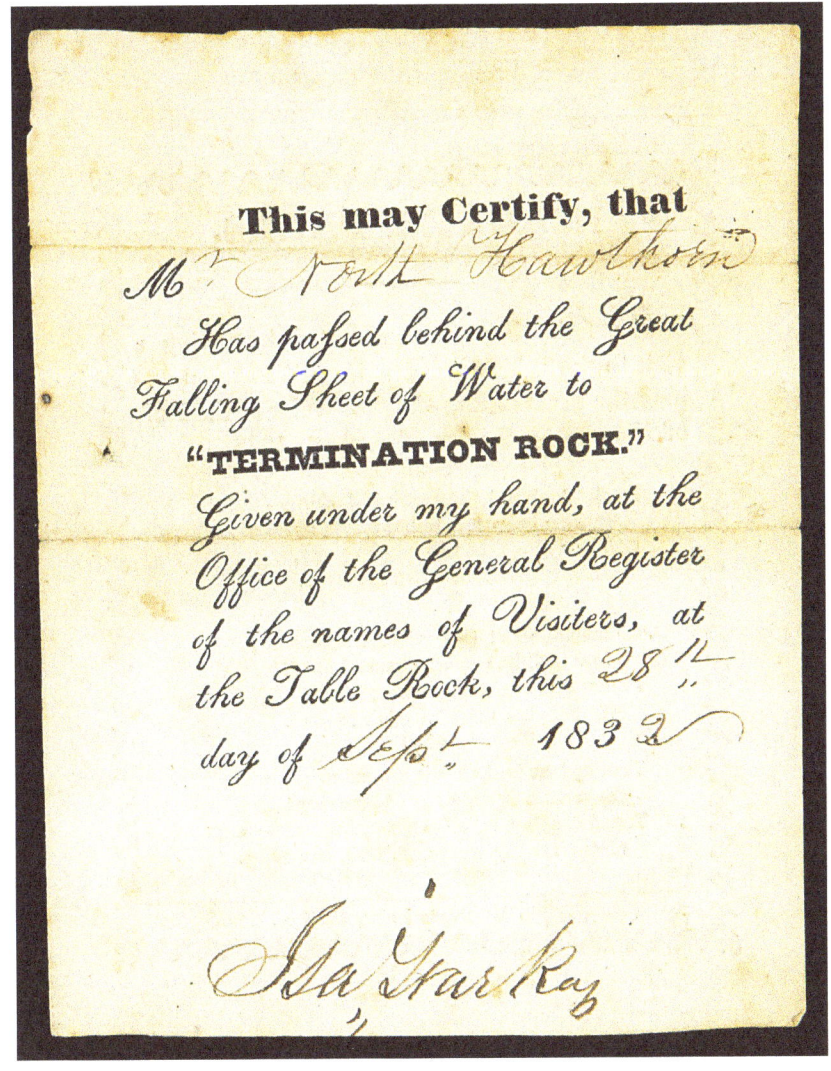

Figure 9. Nathaniel Hawthorne's printed certificate to Niagara Falls (Termination Rock) from 1832. Nathaniel Hawthorne Collection, Yale Collection of American Literature, Beinecke Rare Book and Manuscript Library. Yale University Library.

My contemplations were often interrupted by strangers, who came down from Forsyth's to take their first view of the falls. A short, ruddy, middle-aged gentleman, fresh from old England, peeped over the rock, and evinced his approbation by a broad grin. His spouse, a very robust lady, afforded a sweet example of maternal solicitude, being so intent on the safety of her little boy that she did not even glance at Niagara. As for the child, he gave himself wholly to the enjoyment of a stick of candy. Another traveler, a native American, and no rare character among us, produced a volume of captain Hall's tour, and labored earnestly to adjust Niagara to the captain's description, departing, at last, without one new idea or sensation of his own. The next comer was provided, not with a printed book, but with a blank sheet of foolscap, from top to bottom of which, by means of an ever pointed pencil, the cataract was made to thunder. In a little talk, which we had together, he awarded his approbation to the general view, but censured the position of Goat Island, observing that it should have been thrown farther to the right, so as to widen the American falls, and contract those of the Horse-shoe. Next appeared two traders of Michigan, who declared, that, upon the whole, the sight was worth looking at; there certainly was an immense water-power here; but that, after all, they would go twice as far to see the noble stone-works of Lockport, where the Grand Canal is locked down a descent of sixty feet. They were succeeded by a young fellow, in a home-spun cotton dress, with a staff in his hand, and a pack over his shoulders. He advanced close to the edge of the rock, where his attention, at first wavering among the different components of the scene, finally became fixed in the angle of the Horse-shoe falls, which is, indeed, the central point of interest. His whole soul seemed to go forth and be transported thither, till the staff slipped from his relaxed grasp, and falling down—down—down—struck upon the fragment of the Table Rock.

In this manner, I spent some hours, watching the varied impression, made by the cataract, on those who disturbed me, and returning to unwearied contemplation, when left alone. At length, my time came to depart. There is a grassy foot-path, through the woods, along the summit of the bank, to a point whence a causeway, hewn in the side of the precipice, goes winding down to the ferry, about half a mile below the Table Rock. The sun was near setting, when I emerged from the shadow of the trees, and began the descent. The indirectness of my downward road continually changed the point of view, and showed me, in rich and repeated succession—now, the whitening rapids and the majestic leap of the main river, which appeared more deeply massive as the light departed; now, the lovelier picture, yet still sublime, of Goat Island with its rocks and grove, and the lesser falls, tumbling over the right bank of the St. Lawrence, like a tributary stream; now, the long vista of the river, as it eddied and whirled between the cliffs, to pass through Ontario towards the sea, and everywhere to be wondered at, for this one unrivalled scene. The golden sunshine tinged the sheet of the American cascade, and painted on its heaving spray the broken semicircle of a rainbow, Heaven's own beauty crowning earth's sublimity. My steps were slow, and I paused long at every turn of the descent, as one lingers and pauses, who discerns a brighter and brightening excellence in what he must soon behold no more. The solitude of the old wilderness now reigned over the whole vicinity of the falls. My enjoyment became the more rapturous, because no poet shared it—nor wretch, devoid of poetry, profaned it: but the spot, so famous through the world, was all my own!

Oscar Wilde: Nothing to Declare but Disappointment

(1854–1900)

When Oscar Wilde arrived in North America for a lecture tour in 1882, he had not yet written the popular satirical plays for which he would later be known. It could be said that his witty, if largely disparaging, comments about Niagara Falls helped to make him a celebrity.

When asked by the American customs officer if he had anything to declare when he arrived at the New York harbor from London in 1882, Oscar Wilde supposedly said: "I have nothing to declare except my genius!"[9]

This line was the first of many to garner public attention, whether it was accurately quoted or not, during his trip to America and Canada on a lecture tour.[10] Though he was sometimes harangued by audiences, roasted by reporters, and exploited by advertisers on his tour, Wilde had the last laugh as his witty style secured his fame. (See figure 10.)

In Rochester, New York, on February 7, Wilde was mocked by a group of university students who frequently interrupted his lecture with hisses and groans. It was his sixth speaking engagement that week, and his talks were getting all manner of attention—for good or ill. He was in need of a holiday. After a lecture on contemporary English artistic tastes at the former Academy of Music in Buffalo, New York, Wilde traveled north on the 6:10 p.m. Central Railroad, crossing the border to Niagara Falls, Ontario where he spent the night at the Prospect House, popular for its proximity to and spectacular views of the Falls.

On the morning of February 9, Wilde viewed the cataracts from his veranda. An "impressive tableau!" the *New York Tribune* reported: "Here, Oscar Wilde in his long fur coat; there, Niagara Falls!"[11] Later, Wilde stood at Table Rock, and then, with his valet, rented a carriage and crossed Suspension Bridge to tour the American side. At Cave of the Winds, he put on an oilskin slicker, which he found ugly and hoped his audience would never wear one. His "consolation," however, is that the actress Sarah Bernhardt had done the same on her visit and was even photographed in it.

Though Wilde's whirlwind tour of the Falls lasted only a single day, his witty observations remain part of the character and caricature of that natural wonder. Open any book published on the Falls in recent years and one is sure to find this most memorable of quips:

> Every American bride is taken there, and the sight of the stupendous waterfall must be one of the earliest, if not the keenest, disappointments in American married life.[12]

It was not only the geographic design of the Falls that had apparently disappointed Wilde. "Niagara Falls seems to me to be simply a vast, unnecessary amount of water going the wrong way," he complained to the *New York Tribune*. But it was also the people as much as the place that Wilde found wanting, telling the *New York Times*: "Niagara is a melancholy place filled with melancholy people, who wander about trying to get up that feeling of sublimity, which the guide-books assure them they can do without

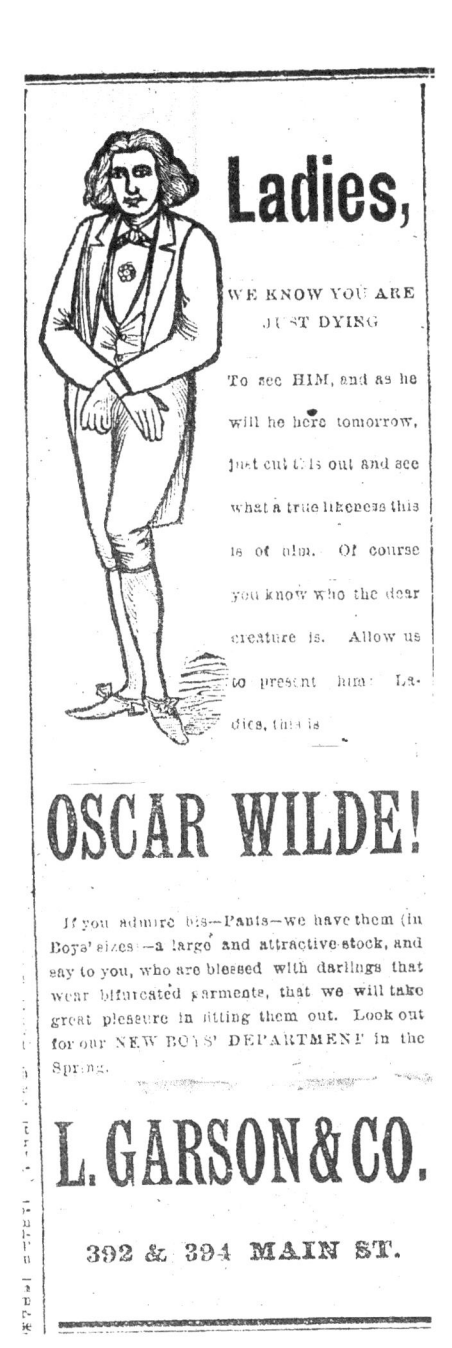

Figure 10. Advertisement. *Buffalo Evening News*, January 31, 1882, to April 27, 1882, NY 96, Box 4 93-31542, New York State Library.

extra charge." Through syndication, Wilde's comments were read across the nation. Not surprisingly, his American audience was not amused.[13]

Nor did Wilde enjoy fellow feeling among his Canadian audiences, despite their imperial relations. Many on both sides of the border saw him as "exotic." To Americans particularly, he was an outsider, a spectacle in velvet knee breeches and fur-trimmed coat, an Oxford dandy who had the audacity to lecture Americans about British tastes and the decorative arts while failing to perceive the beauty of the wonder that was then America's, if not North America's, most iconic and sublime site.

In mock-lyric form, American satirists in the humor magazine *Fun* quickly defended Niagara Falls, publishing the unambiguously titled poem "Disappointed Again" as a response to Wilde's comments. In the poem, the speaker entreats the "Universe," to "improve its old design / Make catastrophes more clever / And phenomena more fine," to appease the blasé Wilde.[14] Perhaps if the Niagara River were dyed pink ("rose-madder"), the lyricists contend, the Aesthete, with his love of the decorative over the natural, might be more impressed.

To a region dependent on tourism, as Niagara Falls certainly was on both sides of the border by the 1880s—each site Wilde visited, including crossing the bridge to Goat Island, would have cost him .50 cents to $1.00 apiece—one can imagine the affront his satiric remarks likely produced among those who made their living on the reputation of the Falls. But this "inventor of modern celebrity,"[15] as Wilde has been called, knew what he was doing. As his most devilish of dandies, Lord Henry Wotton, in his 1895 novel *The Picture of Dorian Gray* later warned: "The only thing worse than being talked about, is *not* being talked about."

Indeed, Wilde's comments did not discourage anyone's interest in the Falls. Three short years after his visit, the first state park in the United States, the Niagara Reservation Park, now the Niagara Falls State Park on the American side, officially opened, welcoming tens of thousands of visitors.[16] The same year, the Niagara Falls Park Act on the Canadian side was established, with the Queen Victoria Park officially opening in 1888. Today, it is estimated that millions of tourists visit the combined Falls annually, in search of escape, entertainment, authenticity, insight, or awe.

In truth, however, Oscar Wilde *wrote* almost nothing about Niagara Falls. Mostly archived in newspaper accounts, Wilde's collected first-person impressions nevertheless resonated with the many who came before and after him, impressions that range from the satirical to the sensory to the spiritual. Wilde encapsulates in a few pithy comments the vast complexity of the Falls, as in an interview with the *Buffalo Express* the day after his visit:

> When I first saw Niagara Falls I was disappointed in the outline. The design, it seemed to me, was wanting in grandeur and variety of line, but the colors were beautiful. The dull gray waters flecked with green are lit with silver, being full of changing loveliness, for of all the most lovely colors are colors in motion. It was not till I stood underneath the Falls at Table Rock that I realized the majestic splendor and strength of the physical forces of nature here. The sight was far beyond what I had ever seen in Europe. It seems to me a sort of embodiment of pantheism.[17]

Wilde's more famous expressions of disappointment, amusing as they are, belie mere dismissiveness then. Even he could not deny the transcendent feel of the Falls, recording in the Prospect Hotel register: "The roar of these waters is like the roar when the mighty wave of democracy breaks against the shores where kings lie couched at ease." Though aspiring to the British society he so satirized in his plays and novel, Wilde was an Irishman, a British subject who identified with the fight against authoritarian rule and convention. He would not be the first to represent the Falls as a symbol of freedom, nor to scale in a single visit a well of disappointment and the peak of reverence. But few would do so in such style.

Chapter 4

Copyrights and Wrongs

*T*oday, the internet makes plagiarism and piracy easier than ever, but new technologies have long presented authors and artists of all media with the challenge of protecting their work. By the mid-nineteenth century, innovations in print technologies—the development of mechanized printing presses; the transition from using labor-intensive movable type to stereotype (plates that allowed for easier print reproduction); the building of paper mills to manufacture wood-pulp paper; and easier book trade due to advances in transportation—generated increased literacy rates and a growing reading public.[1] With easier book publication and circulation and a greater demand, however, the temptation to pirate books outpaced legislation against it. Writers on both sides of the Atlantic faced copyright challenges, including two of the most recognizable names then and now: Charles Dickens and Mark Twain.

Before international copyright agreements, books published by British authors could be reprinted in the US and Canada without the author receiving any of the profits. Unauthorized and pirated copies were sold at much cheaper rates, at a detriment to the author. Conversely, American authors could be pirated abroad, and the works imported into and sold in the US without the author receiving royalties.

For American writers, the Imperial Copyright Act of 1842 (the year of Charles Dickens's visit), provided copyright in British territories (like Canada) so long as the work was *first* published in England. But the rules were fuzzy. In court cases it was determined that to secure legal rights, a writer needed to reside on British soil at the time the work was published in England. For an American writer to secure Imperial copyright, it was understood that a short stay in Canada could secure publication rights in England—and Canada—so long as the work was published in the mother country at the time of the Canadian stay.

After the establishment of the Dominion of Canada (1867), the Canadian Copyright Act of 1875 sought to outweigh the Imperial Copyright Act by requiring residency in Canada to secure copyright privileges there. As Mark Twain soon discovered, international copyright was still not easy to secure. It wasn't until 1891 that the International Copyright Act began to protect American writers publishing abroad, though less so foreign writers publishing in America. Charles Dickens would not reap the copyright benefits Twain had later worked hard to help secure.

Charles Dickens: Boz's Two Cents[2]

(1812–1870)

Charles Dickens first traveled to America in 1842 to try to establish international copyright laws that would help authors gain ownership of and profits from their own work. After his first American tour, however, he ended up losing a friend, losing the respect of some American readers (albeit briefly), and losing money.

On the morning of April 26, 1842, despite a seasick-worthy ride from Cleveland, Ohio across a melting Lake Erie, a trip reminiscent of his rough Atlantic crossing, Charles Dickens immediately sent for a packet of letters from the Buffalo, New York post office upon his arrival to the city. "Our English letters!" he called them. His spirits were lifting.

Signed by fellow British writers, the letters expressed arguments in defense of international copyright laws. Despite his popularity, even by 1842, with novels such as *Oliver Twist* (1837), *Nicholas Nickleby* (1838), and *The Old Curiosity Shop* (1840), Dickens did not receive profits from his American book sales. The absence of international copyright laws left his work unprotected from piracy in America. He thus set out to publish the "English letters" in American newspapers. Though he had been in the United States for nearly five months, he needed the cosigned letters to show that it was not his own self-interest that motivated "sentiments [he had] expressed on all public occasions" since his arrival. Rather, it was a shared sentiment among fellow writers. Nor were British writers alone seeking international copyright protection. His friend Washington Irving had in part convinced Dickens to travel to America to help resolve the matter on American soil.

Over the next few days, while touring Niagara Falls, Dickens sent the letters with well-known English signatures to such publications as the *New York American*, the *New York Express*, and the *Evening Post*. The letters argued that what was really at stake due to the lack of copyright law was the establishment of a national *American* literature. One published letter states:

> Our feeling . . . is not prompted merely by the desire that authors on this side of the Atlantic should obtain some palpable reward of their industry from the mighty Public who enjoy its fruits, but is exalted by the conviction, that, on the issue depends the question, whether the intellect of America shall speedily be embodied in a Literature worthy of its new-born powers, or shall be permitted to languish under disadvantages which may long deprive the world of the full development of its greatness.[3]

To paraphrase: lack of copyright fails not only the author but the public and the nation. It was a sentiment Dickens might have shared with American writers. That is, of course, had he not been so critical of American readers, publishers, and citizens in general.

In a personal letter to his friend and literary executor John Forster, Dickens complains that his popularity has been cheaply bought, for which he has seen none of the profits:

> I seriously believe that it is an essential part of the pleasure derived from the perusal of a popular English book, that the author gets nothing for it. It is so dar-nation 'cute—so knowing in Jonathan[4] to get his reading on those terms. He has the Englishman so regularly on the hip that his eye twinkles with slyness, cunning, and delight; and he chuckles over the humor of the page with an appreciation of it quite inconsistent with, and apart from, its honest purchase. The raven hasn't more joy in eating a stolen piece of meat, than the American has in reading the English book which he gets for nothing.[5]

Dickens's cynicism toward American behavior was not limited to issues of copyright alone. Upon his return to England, he published a narrative of his travels that largely ridiculed American customs and manners, everything from the flimsy look of its towns (it lacked history) to its vulgar humor and idle chatter (among other vile habits, like "spitting"). American readers were offended.

As the *New York Herald* succinctly reported: "With some very few and silly exceptions, the whole American newspaper press is out, hot and heavy, on 'Charles Dickens, Esq.' for the ignorance, bad grammar, bad logic, and bad heart, exhibited in his *brochure* on this country."[6] That "brochure"—Dickens's travel book, *American Notes for General Circulation* (1842)—nevertheless went into multiple editions. It was republished in 1850, 1867, and 1868, each time with a revised Preface. In the 1850 edition, Dickens asks readers whether his judgments have not been justified: "I have nothing to defend, or to explain away," he writes. "The truth is the truth; and neither childish absurdities, nor unscrupulous contradictions, can make it otherwise."[7] There were indeed truths to Dickens's *Notes*, particularly his comments on the hypocrisy, immorality, and violence of slavery, which he had witnessed firsthand in southern states and kept news clippings of throughout his travels. Nevertheless, his otherwise harsh depictions of the American character likely cost him the friendship of Washington Irving.[8]

Dickens toned down the Preface of his later editions of *American Notes*. By his next visit in 1867, Dickens and America had forgiven each other. In a Postscript to the 1868 release of the book, he observes that he has seen "amazing changes" in the few short years since the end of the Civil War. For this, and for the generosity of spirit Americans have shown him, Dickens vows that to any further editions of his books on America, he will append such testimony.[9]

What *did* impress Dickens, both on his first and subsequent visit to America, was Niagara Falls—at least that seen "Upon the English side," as he would put it in a letter to Forster. Shortly after Dickens's arrival in Buffalo on that late April morning in 1842, he boarded a train, heading north in anticipation of the spray and roar he had read about in other travel narratives. Arriving to see "two great white clouds rising up from the depths of the earth," the thirty-year-old Dickens hurried his wife and her maid down a slippery gorge path to board a ferry that would take them across the Niagara River, where he would settle in at the Clifton House Hotel,[10] finally off American soil. The Falls would offer solitude from the *American* public.

A month after Dickens's visit, a Buffalo-based writer published an editorial that did not look kindly on the writer's seclusion:

Buffalo.

Eugene.

Mr. Dickens arrived here in the morning early, took breakfast, and then hastened down to Niagara, without stopping to look at the Falls. He crossed the river at the ferry, and secured lodgings at the Clifton House, and not till then did he appear to take any interest in the grand cataract. I cannot blame him, however, for desiring to stand upon British soil while gazing upon this sublime spectacle. He remained at the Clifton House until Thursday last, when he left for Montreal via Toronto and Kingston. Our citizens were disappointed of seeing him, and many of them incline to think him no "great shakes after all," deeming that his genius ought to be measured by the extent of his respect for their city and them.[11]

Western New Yorkers, like Americans elsewhere, felt the sting of Dickens's snub, and their sentiment was reiterated in reviews of *American Notes*. In one such editorial, an American reviewer had, at least temporarily, the last laugh on Dickens's plea for copyright laws: "It may be stated, as a striking commentary on the ill success of Mr. Dickens's copy-right efforts here, that the book in question [*American Notes*] was published in London, in two volumes, and sold at $5 per copy—then brought to this country, and in 19 hours, issued from the press of the New York New World, at 12 cents per copy."

From *American Notes for General Circulation* (1842)

Chapter XIV: Return to Cincinnati. A Stage Coach Ride from That City to Columbus, and Thence to Sandusky. So, by Lake Erie, to the Falls of Niagara

. . .

There was a gentleman on board, to whom, as I unintentionally learned through the thin partition which divided our state-room from the cabin in which he and his wife conversed together, I was unwittingly the occasion of very great uneasiness. I don't know why or wherefore, but I appeared to run in his mind perpetually, and to dissatisfy him very much. First of all I heard him say: and the most ludicrous part of the business was, that he said it in my very ear, and could not have communicated more directly with me, if he had leaned upon my shoulder, and whispered me: "Boz is on board still, my dear." After a considerable pause he added, complainingly, "Boz keeps himself very close:" which was true enough, for I was not very well, and was lying down, with a book. I thought he had done with me after this, but I was deceived; for a long interval having elapsed, during which I imagine him to have been turning restlessly from side to side, and trying to go to sleep, he broke out again with, "I suppose *that* Boz will be writing a book by-and-by, and putting all our names in it!" at which imaginary consequence of being on board a boat with Boz, he groaned, and became silent.

We called at the town of Erie at eight o'clock that night, and lay there an hour. Between five and six next morning we arrived at Buffalo, where we breakfasted; and, being too near the Great Falls to wait patiently anywhere else, we set off by the train, the same morning at nine o'clock, to Niagara.

It was a miserable day; chilly and raw; a damp mist falling; and the trees in that northern region quite bare and wintry. Whenever the train halted, I listened for the roar; and was constantly straining my eyes in the direction where I knew the Falls must be, from seeing the river rolling on towards them; every moment expecting to behold the spray. Within a few minutes of our stopping, not before, I saw two great white clouds rising up slowly and majestically from the depths of the earth. That was all. At length we alighted: and then, for the first time, I heard the mighty rush of water, and felt the ground tremble underneath my feet.

The bank is very steep, and was slippery with rain and half-melted ice. I hardly know how I got down, but I was soon at the bottom, and climbing, with two English officers who were crossing and had joined me, over some broken rocks, deafened by the noise, half-blinded by the spray, and wet to the skin. We were at the foot of the American Fall. I could see an immense torrent of water tearing headlong down from some great height, but had no idea of shape, or situation, or anything but vague immensity.

When we were seated in the little ferry-boat, and were crossing the swollen river immediately before both cataracts, I began to feel what it was: but I was in a manner stunned, and unable to comprehend the vastness of the scene. It was not until I came on Table Rock, and looked—Great Heaven, on what a fall of bright green water!—that it came upon me in its full might and majesty.

Then, when I felt how near to my Creator I was standing, the first effect, and the enduring one—instant and lasting—of the tremendous spectacle, was Peace. Peace of Mind, tranquility, calm recollections of the Dead, great thoughts of Eternal Rest and Happiness: nothing of gloom or terror. Niagara was at once stamped upon my heart, an Image of Beauty; to remain there, changeless and indelible, until its pulses cease to beat, for ever.

Oh, how the strife and trouble of daily life receded from my view, and lessened in the distance, during the ten memorable days we passed on that Enchanted Ground! What voices spoke from out the thundering water; what faces, faded from the earth, looked out upon me from its gleaming depths; what Heavenly promise glistened in those angels' tears, the drops of many hues, that showered around, and twined themselves about the gorgeous arches which the changing rainbows made!

I never stirred in all that time from the Canadian side, whither I had gone at first. I never crossed the river again for I knew there were people on the other shore, and in such a place it is natural to shun strange company. To wander to and fro all day, and see the cataracts from all points of view; to stand upon the edge of the Great Horse-shoe Fall, marking the hurried water gathering strength as it approached the verge, yet seeming, too, to pause before it shot into the gulf below; to gaze from the river's level up at the torrent as it came streaming down; to climb the neighbouring heights and watch it through the trees, and see the wreathing water in the rapids hurrying on to take its fearful plunge; to linger in the shadow of the solemn rocks three miles below; watching the river as, stirred by no visible cause, it heaved and eddied and awoke the echoes, being troubled yet, far down beneath the surface, by its giant leap; to have Niagara before me, lighted by the sun and by the moon, red in the day's decline, and grey as evening slowly fell upon it; to look upon it every day, and wake up in the night and hear its ceaseless voice: this was enough.

    I think in every quiet season now, still do those waters roll and leap, and roar and tumble, all day long; still are the rainbows spanning them, a hundred feet below. Still, when the sun is on them, do they shine and glow like molten gold. Still, when the day is gloomy, do they fall like snow, or seem to crumble away like the front of a great chalk cliff, or roll down the rock like dense white smoke. But always does the mighty stream appear to die as it comes down, and always from its unfathomable grave arises that tremendous ghost of spray and mist, which is never laid: which has haunted this place with the same dread solemnity since Darkness brooded on the deep, and that first flood before the Deluge—Light—came rushing on Creation at the word of God.

From Table Rock Album (1855)[12]

Niagara—here Nature holds its sway,
While man, with both delight and awe, doth
Gaze and wonder at its magnificence.

                                       Boz.

From Letter excerpts, 1867 trip, included in
The Life of Charles Dickens, Vol. III, by John Forster (1874)

This Buffalo has become a large and important town, with numbers of German and Irish in it. But it is very curious to notice, as we touch the frontier, that the American female beauty dies out; and a woman's face clumsily compounded of German, Irish, Western America, and Canadian, not yet fused together, and not yet moulded, obtains instead. Our show of Beauty at night is, generally, remarkable; but we had not a dozen pretty women in the whole throng last night, and the faces were all blunt. I have just been walking about, and observing the same thing in the streets. . . . The winter has been so severe, that the hotel on the English side at Niagara (which has the best view of the Falls, and is for that reason very preferable) is not yet open. So we go, perforce, to the American: which telegraphs back to our telegram: "all Mr. Dickens's requirements perfectly understood." I have not yet been in more than two *very bad* inns. I have been in some, where a good deal of what is popularly called "slopping round" has prevailed; but have been able to get on very well. "Slopping round," so used, means untidyness and disorder.

. . .

We went everywhere at the Falls, and saw them in every aspect. There is a suspension bridge across, now, some two miles or more from the Horse Shoe; and another, half a mile nearer, is to be opened in July. They are very fine but very ticklish, hanging aloft there, in the continual vibration of the thundering water: nor is one greatly reassured by the printed notice that troops must not cross them at step, that bands of music must not play in crossing, and the like. I shall never forget the last aspect in which we saw Niagara yesterday. We had been everywhere, when I thought of struggling (in an open carriage) up some very difficult ground for a good distance, and getting where we could stand above the river, and see it, as it rushes forward to its tremendous leap, coming for miles and miles. All away to the horizon on our right was a wonderful confusion of bright green and white water. As we stood watching it with our faces to the top of the Falls, our backs were towards the sun. The majestic valley below the Falls, so seen through the vast cloud of spray, was made of rainbow. The high banks, the riven rocks, the forests, the bridge, the buildings, the air, the sky, were all made of rainbow. Nothing in Turner's finest water-colour drawings, done in his greatest day, is so ethereal, so imaginative, so gorgeous in colour, as what I then beheld.

I seemed to be lifted from the earth and to be looking into Heaven. What I once said to you, as I witnessed the scene five and twenty years ago, all came back at this most affecting and sublime sight. . . .

Mark Twain: The Cost of Travel

(1835–1910)

Mark Twain traveled the world in the thirty years between his first and last mentions of Niagara Falls in his travel writing. But it was a trip closer to home that cost him a great deal more than the price of travel. "Stepping over" to neighboring Canada to fulfill the requirements of copyright laws revealed the gulf between words and meaning, expectation and experience, profit and loss.

Mark Twain played a significant role in helping to establish copyright laws still in place today. But he wasn't always the "practical business man" when it came to protecting his work. Twain had a contentious relationship with Canadian publishers who pirated his books throughout the 1870s and 1880s and sold them for less than the authorized editions in the US. He worked hard to get copyright laws in place that would protect against such piracy. He also worked hard to protect his work by other means.

Though arguably most recognized for his novels *The Adventures of Tom Sawyer* (1876) and *Adventures of Huckleberry Finn* (1884), much of Twain's income came from his travel writing. It was a genre he had honed since his start in journalism as a travel correspondent throughout the 1860s when Samuel Langhorne Clemens adopted the pen name "Mark Twain," a mask that allowed him many comic and satiric liberties. Twain's journalistic correspondence would evolve into the best-selling travel book of the nineteenth century, *The Innocents Abroad, or The New Pilgrims' Progress* (1869), a humorous account of his tour to the Old World.

The year of Twain's first great travel writing success happened to coincide with his move to Buffalo, New York, to become editor and partial owner of the *Buffalo Express*, a position he held from 1869 to 1871.[13] Shortly before Twain began his editorship of the *Express*, he traveled to Niagara Falls with his bride-to-be, Olivia Langdon of Elmira, New York, and her family and friends. On August 4, 1869, they registered at the

Cataract House Hotel on the American side of the Falls, though Twain also toured the Canadian side. If Twain's expectation is grandeur, his experience is anything but—or so he says.

In his chronicle of this visit, "A Day at Niagara. Concerning the Falls. The Tamed Hackman," published in the August 21, 1869 edition of the *Buffalo Express*, Twain conveyed the "truth" of his disappointment in the Falls. He complains of all the signs telling "what you must *not* do" and of "so much instruction to keep track of," such as: "Don't climb the trees"; "Visit Cave of the Winds"; "Photographs of the Falls taken here"; and "Don't throw stones down—they may hit people." The photographers are a particular nuisance. Twain laments the "long ranks of photographers standing guard behind their cameras, ready to make an ostentatious frontispiece of you . . . and a diminished and unimportant background of sublime Niagara." Here, and in another article printed a week later, Twain makes the point that tourists look little at the Falls proper. The truth is, it is not the Falls that disappoint, but the people.

Thirty years and many travels after his first visit to Niagara Falls, Twain attempted again to represent this natural wonder. In *Following the Equator*, a lecture tour across North America and the British Empire, Twain asks: How can one describe grandeur, beauty, and sublime feeling for a place? He was trying to describe the magnificence of India's Taj Mahal, and found he could only do so through analogy—to that most iconographic symbol of North America, Niagara Falls. (See figure 11.) The truth is that the first experience of each place typically comes through reading a travel narrative. And reality rarely, if ever, measures up to imagination and expectation.[14]

The Falls are not the equivalent of the "Atlantic ocean pouring down thence over cloud-vexed Himalayan heights," as he's heard. To avoid such disappointing truths then, Twain's recommendation is, "to stay miles away" from such grand sites, to give up travel altogether—but *not* to give up *reading* travel books. Twain needed after all to make his living.

Claiming that he had to visit Niagara Falls fifteen times to judge its grandeur—to achieve what Oscar Wilde had later referred to as "that feeling of sublimity the guidebooks promise"—Twain was supposedly disappointed in the Falls on his first excursion there. Yet this claim in *Following the Equator* appears nearly thirty years after his first visit to the site, suggesting that its initial impression on him was greater than he let on.

Copyrights and Wrongs / 65

THE TAJ MAHAL.

AN EXAGGERATED NIAGARA.

Figure 11. "An Exaggerated Niagara," published in Twain's travel book, *Following the Equator: A Journey around the World*. Hartford, Connecticut: American Pub. Co., 1897. https://catalog.hathitrust.org/Record/001113062.

Despite Twain's arguable awe of Niagara Falls, however, he did not always have an easy publishing relationship with neighboring Canada. Like Charles Dickens, Twain's works were often pirated by Canadian publishers and sold there as well as in the US for much less than his authorized British and American editions. Among the worst instances of piracy impacting Twain was the 1876 Canadian publication of *The Adventures of Tom Sawyer* by the Toronto-based publishing company Belford Brothers. Though their unauthorized edition appeared after the novel's English release (only one month later), it beat Twain's American publication of the book by nearly half a year. Extremely popular, the Canadian print of *Tom Sawyer* sold so well it went into a third edition, though Twain did not see one cent of its profits, costing him tens of thousands of dollars.[15]

To avoid repeat losses, in preparation for the release of his folktale *The Prince and the Pauper* in 1881, Twain began a two-week stay in Montreal, Canada, to establish residence. He had done so often a decade earlier while living in Buffalo.[16] To obtain Canadian rights to royalties, the Canadian Copyright Act of 1875 obliged writers to "domicile" in Canada at the time of publication on Canadian soil. It sounded simple enough, as Twain himself later said to an interviewer: "I always take the trouble to step over in Canada and stand on English soil," he remarked, as if one could just stride across that small border of blue on the map.[17]

Twain thought his copyright would be secure because he was both on "British soil," the day the book was published, and he was fulfilling the residency requirements of Canadian copyright law. His Canadian publishers, Dawson Brothers, had applied for interim copyright to protect from another edition being imported into Canada until the book could also be published in London, where Twain had simultaneously applied for Imperial Copyright. On the application for interim copyright, Dawson Brothers wrote that Twain's "domicile" was Canada. So far, so good.

Once the work was published in London, then, Twain applied for full copyright in Canada. But he made an error on this subsequent application. Otherwise so careful in his calculations to protect ownership of his work, and so precise in his language, he had written "elective domicile" on his second application. He inadvertently created a discrepancy between his interim application and his application for full copyright in Canada to *The Prince and the Pauper*.

Though Twain had arguably fulfilled the requirements of both the Imperial and the Canadian Copyright Acts, it was his claim to residency that was at issue. "Elective domicile," did not mean permanent residency to the Canadian Department of Agriculture, the office in charge of the import of goods. (See figure 12.) As a December 29, 1881 *New York Times* article on the issue put it, elective domicile was "an address or place where it has been agreed that the delivery will be accepted, although it does not follow that the person so electing his domicile there shall ever visit it."[18] Twain did visit it—he "stepped over" into Canada after all—but he did not have a claim to ownership of his own work published there. His travels on this occasion failed to produce profit. With thousands of dollars at stake, Twain likely found that the gulf between word and meaning is not always funny.

From "English Festivities. And Minor Matters. Fishing" in the *Buffalo Express*, August 28, 1869

But seriously, (for it is well to be serious occasionally), Niagara Falls is a most enjoyable place of resort. The hotels are excellent, and the prices not at all exorbitant. . . .

GUIDES, PHOTOGRAPHERS AND SUCH

The weather is cool in summer, and the walks and drives are all pleasant and none of them fatiguing. When you start out to "do" the Falls you first drive down about a mile, and pay a small sum for the privilege of looking down from a precipice into the narrowest part of the Niagara river. A railway "cut" through a hill would be as comely if it had the angry river tumbling and foaming through its bottom. You can descend a staircase here a hundred and fifty feet down, and stand at the edge of the water. After you have done it, you will wonder why you did it; but you will then be too late. The guide will explain to you, in his blood-curdling way, how he saw the little steamer, Maid of the Mist, descend the fearful rapids—how first one paddle-box was out of sight behind the raging billows and then the other, and at what point it was that her smokestack toppled overboard, and where her planking began to break and part asunder—and how she did finally live through the trip, after accomplishing the incredible feat of traveling seventeen miles in six minutes, or six miles in seventeen minutes, I have really forgotten which. But it was very extraordinary, anyhow.

Figure 12. Thomas Nast, "Innocence Abroad (in search of a copyright)," *Harper's Weekly* 26, no. 1308, January 21, 1882, p. 37. One print, wood engraving, AP2.H32 1882, Case Y. Library of Congress Prints and Photographs Division.

It is worth the price of admission to hear the guide tell the story nine times in succession to different parties, and never miss a word or alter a sentence or a gesture.

Then you drive over to Suspension Bridge, and divide your misery between the chances of smashing down two hundred feet into the river below, and the chances of having the railway train overhead smashing down on to you. Either possibility is discomforting taken by itself, but, mixed together, they amount in the aggregate to positive unhappiness. On the Canada side you drive along the chasm between long ranks of photographers standing guard behind their cameras, ready to make an ostentatious frontispiece of you and your decaying ambulance, and your solemn crate with a hide on it, which you are expected to regard in the light of a horse, and a diminished and unimportant background of sublime Niagara; and a great many people have the incredible effrontery or the native depravity to aid and abet this sort of crime. Any day, in the hands of these photographers, you may see stately pictures of papa and mamma, Johnny and Bub and Sis, or a couple of country cousins, all smiling vacantly, and all disposed in studied and uncomfortable attitudes in their carriage, and all looming up in their awe-inspiring imbecility before the snubbed and diminished presentment of that majestic presence whose ministering spirits are the rainbows, whose voice is the thunder, whose awful front is veiled in clouds, who was monarch here dead and forgotten ages before this hackful of small reptiles was deemed temporarily necessary to fill a crack in the world's unnoted myriads, and will still be monarch here ages and decades of ages after they shall have gathered themselves to their blood relations, the other worms, and been mingled with the unremembering dust. There is no actual harm in making Niagara a background whereon to display one's marvelous insignificance in a good strong light, but it requires a sort of superhuman self-complacency to enable one to do it.

Further along they show you where that adventurous ass Blondin,[19] crossed the Niagara river, with his wheelbarrow on a tightrope, but the satisfaction of it is marred by the reflection that he did not break his neck.

A DISMAL EXPERIENCE

When you have examined the stupendous Horse Shoe Fall till you are satisfied you cannot improve on it, you return to America by the new suspension bridge, and follow up the bank to where they exhibit the Cave of the Winds. Here I followed instructions, and divested myself of all my clothing, and put on a waterproof jacket and overalls. This costume is picturesque, but not beautiful. A guide, similarly dressed, led the way down a flight of winding stairs, which wound and wound, and still kept on winding long after the thing ceased to be a novelty, and then terminated long before it had begun to be a pleasure. We were then well down under the precipice, but still considerably above the level of the river. We now began to creep along flimsy bridges of a single plank, our persons shielded from destruction by a crazy wooden railing, to which I clung with both hands—not because I was afraid, but because I wanted to. Presently the descent became steeper, and the bridge flimsier, and sprays from the American Fall began to rain down on us in fast increasing sheets that soon became blinding, and after that our progress was mostly in the nature of groping. Now a furious wind began to rush out from behind the waterfall, which seemed determined to sweep us from the bridge, and scatter us on the rocks and among the torrents below. I remarked that I wanted to go home; but it was too late. We were almost under the monstrous wall of water thundering down from above, and speech was in vain in the midst of such a pitiless crash of sound. In another moment the guide disappeared behind the deluge, and, bewildered by the thunder, driven helplessly by the wind, and smitten by the arrowy tempest of rain, I followed. All was darkness. Such a mad storming, roaring, and bellowing of warring wind and water never crazed my ears before. I bent my head, and seemed to receive the Atlantic on my back. The world seemed going to destruction. I could not see anything, the flood poured down so savagely. I raised my head, with open mouth, and the most of the American cataract went down my throat. If I had sprung a leak now I had been lost. And at this moment I discovered that the bridge had ceased, and we must trust for a foot-hold to the slippery and precipitous rocks. I never was so scared before and survived it. But we got through at last, and emerged into the open day, where we could stand in front of the laced and frothy and seething world of descending water, and look at it. When I saw how much of it there was, and how fearfully in earnest it was, I was sorry I had gone behind it. . . .

From *Following the Equator* (1897)

I had to visit Niagara fifteen times before I succeeded in getting my imaginary Falls gauged to the actuality and could begin to sanely and wholesomely wonder at them for what they were, not what I had expected them to be. When I first approached them it was with my face lifted toward the sky, for I thought I was going to see an Atlantic ocean pouring down thence over cloud-vexed Himalayan heights, a sea-green wall of water sixty miles front and six miles high, and so, when the toy reality came suddenly into view—that beruffled little wet apron hanging out to dry—the shock was too much for me, and I fell with a dull thud.

Yet slowly, surely, steadily, in the course of my fifteen visits, the proportions adjusted themselves to the facts, and I came at last to realize that a waterfall a hundred and sixty-five feet high and a quarter of a mile wide was an impressive thing. It was not a dipperful to my vanished great vision, but it would answer.

I know that I ought to do with the Taj as I was obliged to do with Niagara—see it fifteen times, and let my mind gradually get rid of the Taj built in it by its describers, by help of my imagination, and substitute for it the Taj of fact. It would be noble and fine, then, and a marvel; not the marvel which it replaced, but still a marvel, and fine enough. I am a careless reader, I suppose—an impressionist reader; an impressionist reader of what is not an impressionist picture; a reader who overlooks the informing details or masses their sum improperly, and gets only a large splashy, general effect—an effect which is not correct, and which is not warranted by the particulars placed before me—particulars which I did not examine, and whose meanings I did not cautiously and carefully estimate. It is an effect which is some thirty-five or forty times finer than the reality, and is therefore a great deal better and more valuable than the reality; and so, I ought never to hunt up the reality, but stay miles away from it, and thus preserve undamaged my own private mighty Niagara tumbling out of the vault of heaven, and my own ineffable Taj, built of tinted mists upon jeweled arches of rainbows supported by colonnades of moonlight. It is a mistake for a person with an unregulated imagination to go and look at an illustrious world's wonder.

Chapter 5

Books That Started a War

The Niagara River, with its frontier borders was a critical last passage before the terminus of the Underground Railroad on Canadian soil. Canada's 1793 Act to Limit Slavery[1] outlawed the importation of enslaved people into Upper Canada, and set a course to freedom for those within its borders. That same year, however, the first Fugitive Slave Act passed on the American side of the Niagara River, making enforceable by law the arrest of those seeking freedom and charging a fine to those who helped.

Many northerners resisted the Act. New York State had begun a process of "gradual emancipation" in 1799, fully abolishing slavery in 1827, but visitors to the state could still bring enslaved persons with them without those slaves receiving emancipation, until 1841. But, in 1850, the US Congress strengthened the 1793 Act, heavily fining and criminalizing help given to fugitives and making easier their legal seizure, arrest and reenslavement. For those who made it to New York, the door to liberation was again closing. Making it to Canada was now a matter of urgency.

Harriet Beecher Stowe's best-selling novel *Uncle Tom's Cabin* appeared two years after the Fugitive Slave Act of 1850. Abolitionist novels like Stowe's and "slave narratives" or "freedom narratives" published in the period were powerful arguments for change. Stories of arduous journeys out of captivity appeared as early 1760. By 1830, narratives of slave life, told by former and current enslaved people were regularly printed and read. When antislavery societies were gaining membership and momentum, the recruitment of formerly enslaved and free blacks to tell their stories was a powerful vehicle of abolitionist activism. Literary scholar

John Sekora notes that, "In the years from 1831 to the Emancipation Proclamation, more slave narratives were printed in America than any other literary form."[2] These accounts of life under slavery continued to be written or recorded well after the Civil War (1861–1865), up to and including interviews of formerly enslaved persons in the mid-1930s by the Federal Writer's Project of the Works Progress Administration (WPA).

Many slave narratives were "mediated" by white authors and editors, however, who either transcribed stories dictated by those denied literacy,[3] or who shaped stories in ways that would compel abolitionists, as editors did with the Rev. Josiah Henson's narrative. Such mediation does not extinguish, however, the individual claims to selfhood that recur in slave narratives and thereby collectively bear witness to systematized practices of dehumanization and to courageous acts of personal experience.[4] Telling one's story was not only a way of enacting one's freedom and asserting self-hood—that is one's own authority—it was also an act of resistance in the ongoing struggle to emancipate others. To put it in today's sentiments: slave narratives spoke truth to power.[5]

Harriet Beecher Stowe and Josiah Henson: Fiction and Truth

Harriet Beecher Stowe

(1811–1896)

Harriet Beecher Stowe's written impressions of Niagara Falls are nearly as brief as her visit. Nevertheless, her words endure in popular representations of the Falls.[6] *However, it is her most well-known writing,* Uncle Tom's Cabin, *that bears a much longer connection to the region.*

In the summer of 1834, on a trip to New England, Harriet Beecher boarded a stagecoach in Cincinnati, Ohio, where she listened to passengers dispute slavery. It was an echo of the debates she had witnessed a few months earlier at the progressive Lane Theological Seminary, where Beecher's father was president and her future husband Calvin Stowe was a professor.[7] For over three weeks, young men at Lane deliberated the issue of full emancipation or colonization of enslaved peoples.[8] The previous year, in 1833, Stowe had witnessed slavery firsthand in Kentucky while visiting the family of one of her own students from the Western Female Institute.[9]

After the stagecoach to Toledo, Stowe took a steamer across Lake Erie to Buffalo, then traveled on to Niagara Falls, New York, before departing by riverboat on the Erie Canal. Her stop at the Falls was brief, as is her description of it, composed in a personal letter:

> Let me tell, if I can, what is unutterable. I did not once think whether it was high or low; whether it roared or didn't roar; whether it equaled my expectations or not. My mind whirled off, it seemed to me, in a new, strange world. It seemed unearthly, like the strange dim images in the Revelation. I thought of the great white throne; the rainbow around it; the throne in sight like unto an emerald; and oh! that beautiful water rising like moonlight, falling as the soul sinks when it dies, to rise refined, spiritualized, and pure; that rainbow, breaking out, trembling, fading, and again coming like a beautiful spirit walking the waters. Oh, it is lovelier than it is great; it is like the Mind that made it: great, but so veiled in beauty that we gaze without terror. I felt as if I could have *gone over* with the waters; it would be so beautiful a death; there would be no fear in it. I felt the rock tremble under me with a sort of joy. I was so maddened that I could have gone too, if it had gone.[10]

Like many other writers' experiences of the Falls, Stowe's is a spiritual one. Her account draws on transcendent visions of resurrection, and so it is no wonder that her early biographer, Annie Fields, said of these impressions: "Her style is of the very fibre of her own being, and she lives again for us as we read."[11]

By the time of Stowe's return to Cincinnati, in the fall of 1834, the majority of students at Lane Seminary, who had now formed an antislavery society, had withdrawn in protest of the trustee's ban on further activism. These early debates and the Stowe family's abolitionism would later inform her writing of the best-selling novel of the nineteenth century, *Uncle Tom's Cabin* (1852), about which president Abraham Lincoln is *claimed* to have said: "So, you're the little woman who wrote the book that made this great war!"

The antislavery novel was written in response to the Fugitive Slave Act of 1850. Though Stowe's novel had been serialized in forty-one installments from June 1851 to April 1852, its first day of publication as a complete novel nevertheless sold three thousand copies. By the end of the year, that number had grown to three hundred thousand. The novel was also widely read and praised in Canada. Across the Atlantic, Stowe's readership exploded, with an estimated 1.5 million copies sold in England. It was translated into over twenty languages.

Both then and now, *Uncle Tom's Cabin* was provocative. The book has often rightly been criticized for itsstereotypes, but what is indisputably praised time and again is the emotional intensity of its abolitionist sympathies in portraying the violence of the slavery system. The book further mobilized the antislavery movement. The Fugitive Slave Acts were repealed in 1864.

Like all good historical fiction writers, Stowe researched as she wrote. She kept newspaper clippings of articles related to slavery. She personally knew liberated slaves as well as collaborators in the Underground Railroad. She was an informed reader of slave narratives, including those of Henry Bibb and Frederick Douglass, the latter of whom she had written to in Rochester, New York, to request contact with a former slave, such as Bibb, who might provide details of plantation conditions in the South. And, as she notes in *A Key to Uncle Tom's Cabin; Presenting the Original Facts and documents upon which the Story Is Founded* (1853), accounting for the novel's accuracy in its depiction of enslavement, she read and used as one of her sources for the novel the narrative of Josiah Henson, a fugitive slave living in Canada West (present-day Ontario).

Henson dictated and published his story in 1849 as, *The Life of Josiah Henson, Formerly a Slave, Now an Inhabitant of Canada, as Narrated by Himself*. His earliest memory, at age three, is of seeing his father's bloody body, mutilated at the hands of his Maryland enslaver. The narrative details Henson's own later brutal treatment by an overseer in which his arm and possibly both shoulder blades were broken. After four decades of enslavement, Henson determined on the salvation of the North: "Once to get away with my wife and children, to some spot where I could feel that they were indeed *mine*—where no grasping master could stand between me and them, as arbiter of their destiny—was a heaven yearned after with insatiable longing." That heaven was the "Promised Land": Canada.

Rev. Josiah Henson

(1789–1883)

Just after sundown on a late October evening in 1830, under threat of pursuit by Kentucky scouts, the fugitive slave Josiah Henson put his faith in three crewmen to escort himself, his wife, and their four children on a rowboat from Sandusky, Ohio, to a trading vessel anchored a short distance offshore on Lake Erie. The vessel was bound for Buffalo, New York. Henson had twice before passed up opportunities to escape his forty-two years of enslavement, wanting to achieve liberation by means *he* felt to be morally right.

The first time Henson chose *not* to escape was when he was entrusted to transport, by himself, eighteen other enslaved people, his wife and children included, from Maryland to Kentucky, a trip that took them close to the border of the free state of Ohio. On a later journey back to Maryland, Henson had earned money from preaching to purchase his own freedom, only to have the money stolen by his former enslaver. Unable to pay the "debt" of his own purchase, Henson was to be sold in the dreaded "deep South," but was saved only when the man's nephew became terribly ill, needing Henson to nurse him and return him safely home while traveling by riverboat from Louisiana to Kentucky. Even this noble task would not earn Henson his freedom.

By the fall of 1830, Henson had decided not to let another chance slip past. Providentially, captain and crew on the Lake Erie trading ship were antislavery sympathizers who welcomed the fugitives aboard. Arriving in Buffalo late that October evening, and determining the Niagara River then too dangerous to cross, the vessel sailed early the following morning two miles north to the village of Black Rock, where the captain paid the fare for the Hensons to board a Canadian ferry to Waterloo and to their freedom.

Within four years of his liberation, Henson earned enough money from farming to purchase, jointly with other former slaves, a tract of land for the purpose of building a self-sustaining black community. Within another two years, with the aid of American abolitionist missionaries and supporters, he would establish and become a leader of the Dawn Settlement in Dresden, Canada West (Ontario), where fugitives could settle in their own homes, acquire new skills and education, and make their own livings.

Henson's escape narrative was reissued in 1858, with this curious subtitle: *Truth Stranger Than Fiction. Father Henson's Story of His Own Life.* This time, the autobiography contained something more: *With an Introduction by Mrs. H. B. Stowe.*

Henson's widely read autobiography was published twice more after the 1858 "Truth Stranger Than Fiction" edition, in 1876 and 1881. Though not until very late in life did Henson directly refer to himself as "Uncle

Tom," his editors had done so from the early 1850s onward, despite the fact that it had already become a racial stereotype used by those who opposed abolition. The versions of the life become increasingly bolder, as the later titles attest, identifying Henson *as* "Uncle Tom"—a grasp at fame by his white editor and publisher by linking him to Stowe's novel. Henson was no ghost though, his editor, John Lobb, wrote in the last edition of "Uncle Tom's Story of His Life"—despite the fact that Stowe "*kills* her hero" in the novel. This was a joke Henson himself often used at speeches to raise funds for the Dawn Settlement. The fame Henson received from the publications of the "revised and enlarged" editions of his narrative would peak with his visits to Queen Victoria and president Rutherford B. Hayes.

Unfortunately, Henson would otherwise benefit little from the nearly one million copies sold of "the only authorized edition" of his life, the 1881 edition—by then greatly fabricated and profited from by Lobb, his white editor. As scholar Robin W. Winks notes, what Henson's broader story invites us to remember is not only historical evidence of the fugitive slave's experience, but also the appropriation of that experience and life, and ultimately, "the condition of being black in nineteenth-century North America."[12] Henson had achieved freedom, but he did not always own his own life's story.

> From *The Life of Josiah Henson, Formerly a Slave,*
> *Now an Inhabitant of Canada, as Narrated by Himself*
> (Boston: Arthur D. Phelps, 1849)

In passing over the part of Ohio near the lake, where such an extensive plain is found, we came to a spot overflowed by a stream, across which the road passed. I forded it first, with the help of a sounding-pole, and then taking the children on my back, first, the two little ones, and then the others, one at a time, and, lastly, my wife, I succeeded in getting them all safely across, where the ford was one hundred to one hundred and fifty yards wide, and the deepest part perhaps four feet deep. At this time the skin was worn from my back to an extent almost equal to the size of my knapsack.

One night more was passed in the woods, and of the next forenoon we came out upon the wide plain, without trees, which lies south and west of Sandusky city. We saw the houses of the village, and kept away from them for the present, till I should have an opportunity to reconnoitre a little. When about a mile from the lake, I hid my companions in the bushes, and pushed forward. Before I had gone far, I observed on the left, on the opposite side from the town, something which looked like a house, between which and a vessel, a number of men were passing and repassing with activity. I promptly decided to approach them; and, as I drew near, I was hailed by one of the number, who asked me if I wanted to work. I told him yes; and it was scarcely a minute before I had hold of a bag of corn, which, like the rest, I emptied into the hold of the vessel lying at anchor a few rods off. I got into the line of laborers hurrying along the plank next to the only colored man I saw engaged, and soon entered into conversation with him; in the course of which I inquired of him where they were going, the best route to Canada, who was the captain, and other particulars interesting to me, and communicated to him where I came from, and whither I wished to go. He told the captain, who called me one side, and by his frank look and manner soon induced me to acknowledge my condition and purpose. I found I had not mistaken him. He sympathized with me, at once, most heartily; and offered to take me and my family to Buffalo, whither they were bound, and where they might arrive the next evening, if the favorable wind continued, of which they were hurrying to take advantage. Never did men work with a better will, and soon two or three hundred bushels were thrown on board, the hatches were fastened down, the anchor raised, and the sails hoisted. The captain had agreed to send a boat for me, after sundown, rather than take me on board at the landing; as there were Kentucky spies, he said, on the watch for slaves, at Sandusky, who might get a glimpse of me, if I brought my party out of the bush by daylight. I watched the vessel, as she left her moorings, with intense interest, and began to fear that she would go without me, after all; she stretched off to so great a distance, as it seemed to me, before she rounded to. At length, however, I saw her come up to the wind, and lower a boat for the shore; and, in a few minutes, my black friend and two sailors jumped out upon the beach. They went with me, immediately, to bring my wife and children. But what was my alarm when I came back to the place where I had left them, to find they had gone! For a moment, my fears were overpowering; but I soon discerned them, in the fading twilight, at no great distance. My wife had been alarmed by my long absence, and thought I must have been discovered by some of our watchful enemies, and had given up all for lost. Her fears were not removed by seeing me returning with three other men; and she tried to hide herself. It was not without difficulty that I satisfied her all was right, for her agitation was so great that she could not, at once, understand what I said. However, this was soon over, and the kindness of my companions facilitated the matter very much. Before long, we were all on the way to the boat, and it did not require much time or labor to embark our luggage. A short row brought us to the vessel, and, to my astonishment, we were welcomed on board, with three hearty cheers; for the crew were as much pleased as the captain, with the help they were giving us to escape. A fine run brought us to Buffalo the next evening, but it was too late to cross the river that night. The next morning we dropped down to Black Rock, and the friendly captain, whose name I have gratefully remembered as Captain Burnham, put us on board the ferry-boat to Waterloo, paid the passage money, and gave me a dollar at parting. He was a Scotchman, and had done enough to win my enduring gratitude, to prove himself a kind and generous man, and to give me a pleasant association with his dialect and his country.

  When I got on the Canada side, on the morning of the 28th of October, 1830, my first impulse was to throw myself on the ground, and giving way to the riotous exultation of my feelings, to execute sundry antics which excited the astonishment of those who were looking on. A gentleman of the neighborhood, Colonel Warren, who happened to be present, thought I was in a fit, and as he inquired what was the matter with the poor fellow, I jumped up and told him I was free. "O," said he, with a hearty laugh, "is that it? I never knew freedom make a man roll in the sand before." It is not much to be wondered at, that my certainty of being free was not quite a sober one at the first moment; and I hugged and kissed my wife and children all round, with a vivacity which made them laugh as well as myself. There was not much time to be lost, though, in frolic, even at this extraordinary moment. I was a stranger, in a strange land, and had to look about me at once, for refuge and resource.

Chapter 6

Bridge Traffic

In previous centuries, crossing the US/Canadian border was difficult for geographic reasons—the strong current of the Niagara River, even if not near the rapids above or below the Falls, made for rough crossing in canoes, rafts, and ferries. Easier access across the border began in 1848 with the construction of the Niagara Falls Suspension Bridge—a big idea that began with the small act of flying a kite across the River, first connecting the borders by a string, then rope, then cable. Bridge traffic began with pedestrian and carriage crossing then extended to rail crossing when the bridge was rebuilt in 1855 as the first Railway Suspension Bridge, the stone and iron scaffolding that could transport people by foot or stagecoach in a passageway underneath the train tracks. Mark Twain comically captures what many may have felt about this new structure:

> Then you drive over to Suspension Bridge, and divide your misery between the chances of smashing down two hundred feet into the river below, and the chances of having the railway train overhead smashing down on to you. Either possibility is discomforting taken by itself, but, mixed together, they amount in the aggregate to positive unhappiness.

Written four years after the end of the Civil War and from a place of privilege, Twain had the luxury of satirizing the technological sublime.

Not all could indulge in humor, however. Though New York State had abolished slavery in 1827, the Congressional passing of the 1850

Fugitive Slave Act made crossing the gorge imperative. Canada alone meant freedom. Along the American banks of the Niagara River, those escaping enslavement would wait at hidden "stations" at Niagara Falls, Lewiston, Youngstown, and other neighboring New York towns, waiting for safe passage to this "Promised Land" after long and perilous journeys from Southern states. Alone or with the vital help of others, freedom seekers would cross the River by rowboat, aboard a ferry or steamboat, or on foot or railcar across the Lewiston and Niagara Falls Suspension Bridges, as did Harriet Tubman and her "passengers." It is estimated that thousands of fugitives may have crossed at Niagara before the passing of the Thirteenth Amendment to abolish slavery in 1865.[1]

In the very early years of the twentieth century, the shared border, beauty, and power of the Falls became emblem of the Niagara Movement, an early civil rights movement founded by W. E. B. Dubois, and that later evolved into the National Association for the Advancement of Colored People (NAACP). The first meeting of the Niagara Movement in 1905 took place in Fort Erie, Ontario,[2] with a second to follow in 1906 in Harpers Ferry, Virginia, both locales symbolic in their own ways.

When Walt Whitman crossed the border overlooking the Falls, it stirred his spirit, as it did for Tubman. Niagara Falls had long represented democratic currents against tyranny, a symbol worth recalling as border crossing still presents a peril for many.

Harriet Tubman: "The Line of Danger"

(c. 1820–1913)

A year after the first Railway Suspension Bridge was built in 1855 at Niagara Falls, Harriet Tubman would use the metaphor of the Underground Railroad to literal effect, leading slaves to freedom on a train across the international border.

While the formerly enslaved Rev. Josiah Henson's autobiography of his escape to Canada was being published and read in 1849, Harriet Tubman (born Amarinta Ross) became a fugitive, escaping her Maryland enslavement alone and arriving in a free Philadelphia after a difficult journey. Her name would soon become synonymous with that network of free black, fugitive, and white abolitionists who would provide safe houses, transport, and other resources to assist escaped slaves. Tubman escorted at least seventy fugitives to freedom over the course of ten years and as many dangerous trips to the South.[3] These selfless rescues of her family and others out of bondage earned Tubman the nickname "Moses." Tubman helped to settle refugees in St. Catharines, Canada West (Ontario), where she and her family lived in the 1850s.[4]

When the Fugitive Slave Act in America was enforced a year after Tubman forged her own path to freedom, she is reported by her biographer, Sarah Bradford, to have said: "I wouldn't trust Uncle Sam wid my people no longer, but I brought 'em all clar off to Canada." Though the dialect in which Bradford records Tubman's speech has since come under criticism, the biography preserves—albeit in mediated form through Bradford—some of Tubman's first-person storytelling voice and style, not otherwise available. Tubman herself was unable to read and write. Denied access to literacy as an enslaved person, Tubman inherited an oral tradition. She used performance storytelling to testify to slavery's injustices, to mobilize abolitionists, to express her spiritual visions, to make a living, and even, to entertain.

In *Scenes in the Life of Harriet Tubman* (1869), Bradford tells a story from November 1856 of Tubman taking a group of escaped slaves to freedom by train. Tubman's common routes to the Niagara border were via Elmira, New York (from Pennsylvania), or via New York City and Albany through Syracuse and Rochester, New York. Tubman used the Niagara Falls Suspension Bridge, which had begun accommodating rail crossing only a year earlier.[5] The November 1856 journey included Josiah "Joe" Bailey for whom a $2,000 reward was advertised. Joe, with his brother William and others, were close to recapture.

In the second edition of Tubman's narrative, *Harriet: The Moses of Her People* (1886), Bradford revised the ending of Joe's journey, originally published in *Scenes in the Life of Harriet Tubman*. In the earlier version, the Falls play a more prominent role in Tubman's account, suggesting the more entertaining and playful side to Tubman's storytelling. "Only one more journey for me now, and dat is to Hebben!" Joe is reported to have said upon their arrival in Canada. To which, Tubman replies:

> "Well, you ole fool you," said Harriet, with whom there seems but one step from the sublime to the ridiculous, "you might a' looked at de Falls fust, and den gone to Hebben afterwards." She has seen Joe several times since, a happy and industrious freeman in Canada.[6]

Bridge Traffic / 87

Perhaps it is the criticism of Tubman implied in the line "but one step from the sublime to the ridiculous" that Bradford had thought better of nearly twenty years later. Tubman's story, however, conveys the power of the Falls at the crest of the Suspension Bridge—its glory as symbol of freedom.

<blockquote>
From Harriet: The Moses of Her People by
Sarah H. Bradford (New York:
Geo. R. Lockwood & Son, 1886)
</blockquote>

They finally reached New York in safety: and this goes almost without saying, for I may as well mention here that of the three hundred and more fugitives whom Harriet piloted from slavery, not one was ever recaptured, though all the cunning and skill of white men, backed by offered rewards of large sums of money, were brought into requisition for their recovery.

As they entered the anti-slavery office in New York, Mr. Oliver Johnson rose up and exclaimed, "Well, Joe, I am glad to see the man who is worth $2,000 to his master." At this Joe's heart sank. "Oh, Mas'r, how did you know me!" he panted. "Here is the advertisement in our office," said Mr. Johnson, "and the description is so close that no one could mistake it." And had he come through all these perils, had he traveled by day and night, and suffered cold and hunger, and lived in constant fear and dread, to find that far off here in New York State, he was recognized at once by the advertisement? How, then, was he ever to reach Canada?

"And how far off is Canada?" he asked. He was shown the map of New York State, and the track of the railroad, for more than three hundred miles to Niagara, where he would cross the river, and be free. But the way seemed long and full of dangers. They were surely safer on their own tired feet, where they might hide in forests and ditches, and take refuge in the friendly underground stations; but here, where this large party would be together in the cars, surely suspicion would fall upon them, and they would be seized and carried back. But Harriet encouraged him in her cheery way. He must not give up now. "De Lord had been with them in six troubles, and he would not desert them in de seventh." And there was nothing to do but to go on. As Moses spoke to the children of Israel, when compassed before and behind by dangers, so she spake to her people, that they should "go forward."

Up to this time, as they traveled they had talked and sung hymns together, like Pilgrim and his friends, and Joe's voice was the loudest and sweetest among them; but now he hanged his harp upon the willows, and could sing the Lord's songs no more.

"From dat time," in Harriet's language, "Joe was silent; he talked no more; he sang no more; he sat wid his head on his hand, an' nobody could 'rouse him, nor make him take any intrust in anything."

They passed along in safety through New York State, and at length found themselves approaching the Suspension Bridge. They could see the promised land on the other side. The uninviting plains of Canada seemed to them,

> "Sweet fields beyond the swelling flood,
> All dressed in living green;"

but they were not safe yet. Until they reached the center of the bridge, they were still in the power of their pursuers, who might at any pause enter the car, and armed with the power of the law, drag them back to slavery. The rest of the party were happy and excited; they were simple, ignorant creatures, and having implicit trust in their leader, they felt safe when with her, and no immediate danger threatened them. But Joe was of a different mould. He sat silent and sad, always thinking of the horrors that awaited him if recaptured. As it happened, all the other passengers were people who sympathized with them, understanding them to be a band of fugitives, and they listened with tears, as Harriet and all except poor Joe lifted up their voices and sang:

> I'm on the way to Canada,
> That cold and dreary land,
> De sad effects of slavery,
> I can't no longer stand;
> I've served my Master all my days,
> Widout a dime reward,

> And now I'm forced to run away,
> To flee de lash, abroad;
> Farewell, ole Master, don't think hard of me,
> I'm traveling on to Canada, where all de slaves are free.
> De hounds are baying on my track,
> Ole Master comes behind,
> Resolved that he will bring me back,
> Before I cross the line;
> I'm now embarked for yonder shore,
> Where a man's a man by law,
> De iron horse will bear me o'er,
> To "shake de lion's paw";

Oh, righteous Father, wilt thou not pity me,
And help me on to Canada, where all de slaves are free.

> Oh I heard Queen Victoria say,
> That if we would forsake,
> Our native land of slavery,
> And come across de lake;
> Dat she was standing on de shore,
> Wid arms extended wide,
> To give us all a peaceful home,
> Beyond de rolling tide;
> Farewell, ole Master, don't think hard of me,
> I'm traveling on to Canada, where all de slaves are free.

No doubt the simple creatures with her expected to cross a wide lake instead of a rapid river, and to see Queen Victoria with her crown upon her head, waiting with arms extended wide, to fold them all in her embrace. There was now but "one wide river to cross," and the cars rolled on to the bridge. In the distance was heard the roar of the mighty cataract, and now as they neared the center of the bridge, the falls might be clearly seen. Harriet was anxious to have her companions see this wonderful sight, and succeeded in bringing all to the windows, except Joe. But Joe still sat with his head on his hands, and not even the wonders of Niagara could draw him from his melancholy musings. At length as Harriet knew by the rise of the center of the bridge, and the descent immediately after, the line of danger was passed; she sprang across to Joe's side of the car, and shook him almost out of his seat, as she shouted, "Joe! you've shook de lion's paw!" This was her phrase for having entered on the dominions of England. But Joe did not understand this figurative expression. Then she shook him again, and put it more plainly, "Joe, you're in Queen Victoria's dominions! You're a free man!"

Then Joe arose. His head went up, he raised his hands on high, and his eyes, streaming with tears, to Heaven, and then he began to sing and shout:

"Glory to God and Jesus too,
One more soul got safe;
Oh, go and carry the news,
One more soul got safe."

"Joe, come and look at the falls!"
"Glory to God and Jesus too,
One more soul got safe."

"Joe! it's your last chance. Come and see de falls!"
"Glory to God and Jesus too,
One more soul got safe."

And this was all the answer. The train stopped on the other side; and the first feet to touch British soil, after those of the conductor, were those of poor Joe.

Loud roared the waters of Niagara, but louder still ascended the Anthem of praise from the overflowing heart of the freeman. And can we doubt that the strain was taken up by angel voices and echoed and re-echoed through the vaults of heaven:

Glory to God in the highest,
Glory to God and Jesus too
For all these souls now safe.

"The white ladies and gentlemen gathered round him," said Harriet, "till I couldn't see Joe for the crowd, only I heard his voice singing, 'Glory to God and Jesus too,' louder than ever." A sweet young lady reached over her fine cambric handkerchief to him, and as Joe wiped the great tears off his face, he said, "Tank de Lord! dere's only one more journey for me now, and dat's to Hebben!" As we bid farewell to Joe here, I may as well say that Harriet saw him several times after that, a happy and industrious freeman in Canada.

Walt Whitman: Suspended in Time

(1819–1892)

Walt Whitman visited Niagara Falls two times over thirty years apart, but the most sustained effect on him was written after only "five minutes' perfect absorption" standing on the platform of a train crossing Suspension Bridge in 1880.

Walt Whitman found the waters of Lake Erie, though "beautiful and rare," surprisingly rough, even in the summer months. It was mid-June 1848, and he was on his way home to New Jersey after a brief newspaper stint in New Orleans. Traveling with his brother, the two embarked on a sweeping route across the Great Lakes and Lower Canada. It was his first visit to Niagara Falls. Though he kept notes of his travels in this period, he would not publish them until 1887, after his second visit to the Falls in 1880. His earlier impressions note that the trip across Lake Erie:

> is rougher than it was on Michigan or Huron: (on St. Clair it was smooth as glass;) and our boat rolls a little.—Whether it be from this cause, I don't know, but I feel rather unwell.— The day is bright and dry, with a stiff head wind.—We shall doubtless be in Buffalo this evening.—I anticipate a great deal of pleasure in viewing the Falls of Niagara.—(By Wednesday night I expect to be home.)

The water of Lake Erie looked like Michigan, the morning we started out of Chicago—that bright, lively, blue color, so beautiful and rare.—

We arrived in Buffalo on Monday evening, spent that night and a portion of the next day in examining the place.—In the morning of the next day, got in the cars and went out to Niagara.—Great God! what a sight!—We went under the Falls, saw the whirlpool, and all the other things, including the suspension bridge.—

On Tuesday evening we started for Albany; and travelled all night.—From the time daylight afforded us a view of the country, found it very rich and well cultivated.—Every few miles there were large towns and villages.—[7]

On that 1848 trip, Whitman was likely gathering impressions that would later inform poems in his famous collection *Leaves of Grass*, first published in 1855, but amended and subsequently reprinted as "new" editions five times over the course of his life. Whitman was "afoot with [his] vision," as he put it in "Song of Myself," the *Leaves of Grass* poem that would break new ground in its poetic form—a free verse, sweeping in its scope, that mirrored the spirit of the nation.

Niagara was part of this vision, part of the American landscape, like its prairies and mountains. But this landscape also included people of all walks of life: the old, young, foolish and wise; carpenters, machinists, peddlers, and presidents; Native American, "the hounded slave," soldier, citizen, teacher, and learner. It was a vast, diverse, democratic "new world" Whitman celebrated in his poetry: "Aware of / mighty Niagara," he wrote in 1860, "I strike up for a New World."[8]

That landscape quickly changed, however, with the start of the Civil War. Whitman recounts this change in his 1865 poems of lament, such as "Rise O Days from Your Fathomless Deeps," published in the "Drum Taps" addition to *Leaves of Grass*. Here, the mighty flow of Niagara cannot compare to the human spirit:

Rise O days from your fathomless deeps, till you loftier, fiercer sweep,

Long for my soul hungering gymnastic I devour'd what the earth gave me,
Long I roam'd the woods of the north, long I watch'd Niagara pouring,

Inspired by the democratic spirit of the nation, Whitman traveled its lands, but now, in this moment, that spirit was conflicted. The poet later continues: "Something for us is pouring now more than Niagara pouring."[9] Whitman felt strongly about that "something"—whether it was the devastation he witnessed in field hospitals where he comforted wounded soldiers, or the spirit of human freedom that united a movement. It was a current stronger than Niagara's.[10]

Though Niagara Falls would resurface elsewhere in his writing, only once did it appear—by itself—noteworthy to Whitman: "Great God! what a sight," he had written in 1848. In the published version, included in the collection *November Boughs* (1888), Whitman omits this exclamation, or mention of the newly constructed Suspension Bridge, a structure perched high above the gorge, which must itself have looked a sight.

In Whitman's poetry, Niagara was metaphor—emblematic, like other vistas, of all that America represented. From his June 4, 1880, view, suspended above the earth on stone and steel, Niagara was "complete in all its varied, full, indispensable surroundings." Part of the geographical and symbolic landscape, the Falls inspired something beyond themselves, transcending the present. In this suspension of time, the Falls connect Whitman to other memories and moments of meaning and insight in his life.

That year, on his return trip across the border heading home after a three thousand-mile summer Canadian tour via the Great Lakes, Whitman stayed a night in Niagara Falls, on the American side, with his longtime love, Peter Doyle. He wrote several letters from the Falls, dated September 28, 1880.[11] Having suffered two strokes in the preceding decade and a recent illness, Whitman mentions in the letters that he feels in good health, better than he had in years. His sentiments captured in an earlier "Letter" to the Philadelphia Press and syndicated elsewhere of "five minutes' perfect absorption" in the Falls express nothing less. (See figure 13.)

From *Specimen Days*, "Seeing Niagara to Advantage"

June 4, '80.—For really seizing a great picture or book, or piece of music, or architecture, or grand scenery—or perhaps for the first time even the common sunshine, or landscape, or

Walt Whitman on Seeing Niagara.

For really seizing a great picture, or book, or piece of music, or architecture, or grand scenery—or perhaps for the first time even the common sunshine, or landscape, or maybe the mystery of identity, most curious mystery of all—there comes now and then some lucky five minutes of a man's life, set amid a fortuitous concurrence of circumstances, and bringing in a brief flash the culmination of years of reading and travel and thought. The present case about two o'clock this afternoon gave me Niagara, its superb severity of action and color and majestic grouping (like some colossal cluster of Greek statuary) in one short, indescribable show. We were very slowly crossing suspension bridge—not a full stop anywhere, but next to it—the day clear, sunny, still, and I out on the platform. The falls were in plain view about a mile off, but very distinct, and no roar—hardly a murmur. The river, tumbling green and white, far below me; the dark, high banks, the plentiful umbrage, many bronze cedars, in shadow and tembering and arching all this immense materiality, a clear sky overhead, with a few white clouds, limpid, spiritual, silent. Brief, and as quiet as brief, that picture; yet a remembrance always afterward.

Such are the things, indeed, I lay away with my life's rare and blessed hits of hours, mostly reminiscent, past—the wild sea-storm I once saw one winter day off Fire Island—the elder Booth in Richard that famous night forty years ago in the Old Bowery, or Alboni in the children's scene in Norma, or night views. I remember, on the field after battles in Virginia—or the peculiar sentiment of moonlight and stars over the great plains, Western Kansas—or scooting up New York bay, with a stiff breeze and a good yacht, off Navesink. With these, I say, I henceforth place that view that afternoon, that combination complete, that five minutes perfect absorption of Niagara—not the great majestic gem alone by itself, but set complete in all its varied, full, indispensible surroundings.—*Letter to Philadelphia Press.*

Figure 13. "Walt Whitman on Seeing Niagara," *Newtown Bee*, Newtown, Connecticut, 1877–current, July 14, 1880. Image 1. Image provided by the Connecticut State Library, Hartford, CT, Chronicling America.

maybe even the mystery of identity, most curious mystery of all—there comes some lucky five minutes of a man's life, set amid a fortuitous concurrence of circumstances, and bringing in a brief flash the culmination of years of reading and travel and thought. The present case about two o'clock this afternoon, gave me Niagara, its superb severity of action and color and majestic grouping, in one short, indescribable show. We were very slowly crossing the Suspension bridge—not a full stop anywhere, but next to it—the day clear, sunny, still—and I out on the platform. The falls were in plain view about a mile off, but very distinct, and no roar—hardly a murmur. The river tumbling green and white, far below me; the dark high banks, the plentiful umbrage, many bronze cedars, in shadow; and tempering and arching all the immense materiality, a clear sky overhead, with a few white clouds, limpid, spiritual, silent. Brief, and as quiet as brief, that picture—a remembrance always afterwards. Such are the things, indeed, I lay away with my life's rare and blessed bits of hours, reminiscent, past—the wild sea-storm I once saw one winter day, off Fire island—the elder Booth in Richard, that famous night forty years ago in the old Bowery—or Alboni in the children's scene in Norma—or night-views, I remember, on the field, after battles in Virginia—or the peculiar sentiment of moonlight and stars over the great Plains, western Kansas—or scooting up New York bay, with a stiff breeze and a good yacht, off Navesink. With these, I say, I henceforth place that view, that afternoon, that combination complete, that five minutes' perfect absorption of Niagara—not the great majestic gem alone by itself, but set complete in all its varied, full, indispensable surroundings.

Chapter 7

Words of Art

Can words or images better capture the Falls? "Already you see the world-famous green, baffling painters, baffling poets, shining on the lip of the precipice," wrote Henry James in 1871. That "already" represented nearly two centuries since the first *written* experience of the Falls had been published by Fr. Louis Hennepin in the late seventeenth century, from which the first *illustration* of the Falls was created. Since then, artists, like writers, have tried to represent this wonder of the natural world. No small task that, as even Hennepin's written depiction of the Falls, and its visual accompaniment—sketched only from Hennepin's words rather than the first-person experience of the Dutch artist who had not traveled to see it—have been found to exaggerate its scale and characteristics.[1]

Occasionally, writers tested their skills not only in words but in their own *visual* sketches of the Falls, as did Washington Irving. (See figure 5, chapter 2.) Sometimes writers and artists were close friends, such as James Fenimore Cooper and Thomas Cole, the Hudson River School painter whose images of the Falls are among the most famous. More often, it seems, writers encountered artists at the Falls. Nathaniel Hawthorne, Margaret Fuller, Anthony Trollope, and William Dean Howells all make mention of seeing artists at work during their visits. Trollope's encounter with an artist highlights a friendly competition in the skills and tools of representation. Trollope writes:

> I came across an artist at Niagara who was attempting to draw the spray of the waters. "You have a difficult subject," said I. "All subjects are difficult," he replied, "to a man who desires to

do well." "But yours, I fear is impossible," I said. "You have no right to say so till I have finished my picture," he replied. . . . I began to reflect whether I did not intend to try a task as difficult in describing the falls. . . .

Like Trollope, William Dean Howells and Henry James make an attempt to describe in words what they saw and felt at the Falls. Though friends, their styles could not be more different. Howells finds he can only "suggest" the Falls. With tongue-in-cheek, he asks, "Shall I add myself to the number of absurd people who have attempted to describe Niagara?" It is left to James to illustrate, who perceived that "the line of beauty" had been drawn "on the brow of Niagara."

William Dean Howells: "O feeble pen"

(1837–1920)

William Dean Howells claimed on his first visit to the Falls in 1860 that "no writing and no picture has ever presented them to you." Howells would know. In 1860, he tried to see the Falls through the eyes of well-known artists. A decade later, he fictionalized a visit to the Falls in his first novel.

A young William Dean Howells arrived in Niagara Falls, New York, by train in July 1860. He had just completed a campaign biography of Abraham Lincoln and was on his way to Boston, Massachusetts, on a journalist's mission to research manufacturing in the east. In time he would meet the editors of the *Atlantic Monthly*[2] and eventually writers like Nathaniel Hawthorne, Ralph Waldo Emerson, and Henry David Thoreau. Over the subsequent decade he would be offered the position of assistant editor at the *Atlantic*, and, in 1871, editor. He would also meet and form lasting friendships with Henry James and Mark Twain. For the moment, however, in 1860, he was chronicling his travels from his hometown of Jefferson, Ohio (which he refers to as "Anywhere, Nowhere, Ohio") to Boston, including a stop at the Falls. In his letters for the *Ohio State Journal*, Howells mixes humor with the sublime, satirizing those who intrude on his experiences. The exceptions to his satire were well-known artists he met at the Falls. Here was a challenge—how to sketch the Falls in writing as others could do in art. The manufacturing book he was supposed to write never materialized.

Howells's first letter from the Falls is an exuberant—if somewhat exaggerated, even tongue-in-cheek—description of his impressions. His overly elevated language tries to "tell it," but he finds words to be inadequate—his pen "feeble." What is more, after his initial tour of the Falls, when he returns to his room at the Cataract House Hotel, which he had checked into on July 17, 1860, he reads in the guidebook that he "did" the Falls all wrong! (See figure 14.)

Fortunately, Howells ran into the artist Godfrey Frankenstein the next morning, who helped him to "do" the Falls properly.[3] If, at first, Howells believed that "no pigment can counterfeit" the Falls, Godfrey Frankenstein disproved that to him. Frankenstein was by then famous for exhibiting in 1853 the largest moving panorama of the Falls. Moving panoramas had been created as early as 1828, when William Dunlap used one in his play *A Trip to Niagara*.[4] Soon after Godfrey Frankenstein's own first visit to the Falls in 1844, he began sketching it on canvas. Over the remainder of that decade and into the early years of the next, he painted nearly two hundred scenes of Niagara, at different times of the year, in all types of weather. Reportedly, he even painted in temperatures so frigid, "the spray froze upon the canvas and had to be removed with a knife."[5] From smaller images, the artist magnified one hundred onto gigantic canvases wound on to large rollers to create a visually "moving" Niagara. Audiences flocked to it along the East Coast from New York City to Savannah, Georgia, and as far west as St. Louis, Missouri. If viewers could not travel to the landscape itself, this traveling replica was the next best thing, even evoking feelings of the sublime.[6]

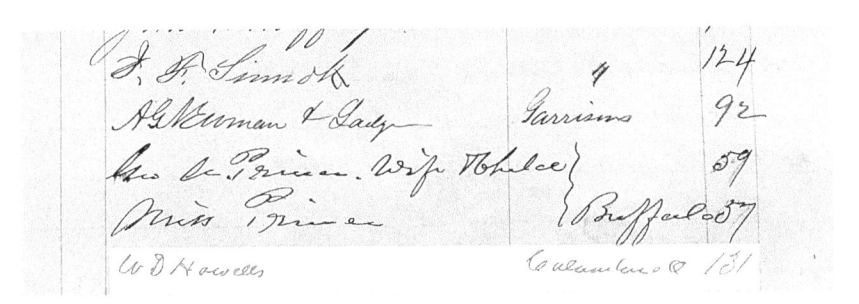

Figure 14. William Dean Howells's Cataract House Hotel registration, July 17, 1860. Cataract House Register, August 1859 to November 1861. Niagara Falls Public Library.

Godfrey, with his brother, the artist John Frankenstein, helped Howells to see the Falls differently—certainly different to how the guidebooks directed him, and he lamented that Godfrey cannot be a guide for all tourists. In "Niagara First and Last," a later essay written for *The Niagara Book* (1893), a collection that included work by his then good friend Mark Twain, Howells admits, however, that he did not see the forms and colors the Godfreys pointed out during that 1860 chance encounter:

> I tried to look at Niagara as actively and pervasively iridescent as they did. They invited me to criticise their pictures in the presence of the facts, and I did once intimate that I failed to find all those rainbows, of different sizes and shapes which they had represented on the surface of the water everywhere. Then they pointed the rainbows out with their forefingers and asked, Didn't I see them there, and there, and there? I looked very hard, and as I was not going to be outdone in the perception of beauty, I said that I did see them.

Howells wasn't quite truthful about who can better perceive the beauty of the Falls, the writer or the artist. This fiction served him well a decade later when he wrote the popular novel *Their Wedding Journey*, begun after his visit with his wife in 1870. The novel was first serialized in the *Atlantic*, and from the first installment won a growing body of readers. It was issued as a book in December 1871 and sold out before Christmas. A special edition, tied with a white ribbon, helped to market the novel as a gift to brides, who might be thinking about traveling to "the honeymoon capital."[7] Howells seemed to have learned something from the spectacles he witnessed at the Falls in 1860 as well. Ultimately he knew that neither writing nor art could render "that profound and subtle magnificence that makes itself felt in the actual presence."

From "En Passant," *The Ohio State Journal*,
Tuesday, July 24, 1860

Niagara Falls, July 17, 1860.

I thought, when I came to see the Falls, I should find myself doubly at a loss for a companion of voyage—for some one to burst forth to. But it was not so. It is true that at the first glance, when I beheld the passionate turmoil of the rapids, as the omnibus whirled me from the depot to the Cataract House, I wanted to confide an emotion or two to the driver; but the thing was impossible; and when afterwards, I descended that interminable tunnel staircase, and stood at the foot of the American Falls, in the real presence of the Cataract—my feeling was that of such repression that it was a divine rapture to remain dumb. It seemed such a feeble and foolish thing to try to speak; not merely on account of the audible voice of the waters, for I could raise my own above that, and make myself heard two feet away. But one could not speak above the tumult of his own soul, to make his voice heard in that of another soul, and so silence seemed wisest, and humblest and best.

There were two women down there, with parasols, and irrepressible skirts and pretty feet, and two gentlemen descended with me. One of these assisted the ladies over the sharp and slippery stones, so bare and shaggy beyond the spray, and so green and grassy within the fall of mist. The other gentleman, who had a clerical aspect, clambered off upon the rocks, as nimble as any goat. For my part, I could only stand still and look at that sublime Revelation, and feel the truth of God. Ah, no words can tell it, no pigment can counterfeit it—that magnificence of whirling, knolled, bewildered, mad, white plunging water, bathed and halved again in snowy mist, almost to the fatal brink from which it leaps. How it furiously combats with itself in the descent, and breaks itself into detached masses, and plunges thundering into the gulf below! How it cries aloud with the strong voice of its agony to the Everlasting. How it crawls frightened, stunned, and bruised, to foam dizzily away from the bottom of the precipice. How the human soul responds to all in those mute wander-words of helpless lulling.

> "Break, break, break,
> At the foot of thy stones, O sea;
> And I would that my tongue could utter
> The thoughts that arise in me."[8]

"Splendid, isn't it?" asked the gentleman who had done the gallant to the ladies, and now stood at my elbow. "And here it has been going for years and years, and doesn't appear to have worn away the rocks at all."

O idle and inadequate wretch!

. . .

I found on returning to my hotel, and looking at my guide book, that I was all wrong to visit Goat Island first—that I ought first to have viewed the cataract from Prospect Point, on the American side. Now, as I am a conscientious and conservative person, and like to do everything in the legitimate way, this grieved me so I immediately hastened to Prospect Point, to repair my error, if possible. Everything is so stupendous in Nature, here, that one is keenly alive to the inadequacy of human life and human affairs—one cannot bear to see a battered tin cup or an old castaway boot, when the voice of Niagara thunders to him; and I was inexpressibly shocked to read on the plank walk leading to Prospect Point: "Go to Jones if you want cheap groceries."

Jones, indeed! Groceries—fie! I would not buy of that wretched man, though he sold to me at cost, and gave me credit.

It was almost dusk when I did Prospect Point, and I returned weary with splendor and magnificence—too weary to glow in the mention of Prospect Point. It is already night. From my window I behold the rapids, dark and headlong; on the heavy air rises hoarsely the thunder of the cataract.

Peace! O feeble pen.

July 18th.—I was very glad to meet Godfrey Frankenstein, the artist, this morning. Under his guidance, I did Goat Island thoroughly, and subtly, and profoundly. The artist at Niagara, like the maker of hay, works most profitably while the sun shines; and this forenoon, when some light clouds had dimmed the sun, my painter-friend put up the beautiful sketch which he was making of the Canada *Fall*, and we started together upon the circuit of the island.

Ah! if this man could waste his time as guide, how gloriously the public could see Niagara. For I penetrated with him all manner of inscrutable thickets and secret nooks, commanding unknown views of the cataract—places that only an artist's eye could discover. He taught me, too, to see some of the beautiful tints of the water and mists—delicious purples, and greens and crimsons—that escape the greedy, common eye, which gulps and bolts the whole thing, as it were, untasted. Sixteen summers' sojourn about Niagara has made Frankenstein intimate with all its beauties, and he seems in some sort the genius of the place, and worthy, if any one is worthy, to paint it. He takes you down a narrow path, steeply dropping through the hillside cedars, where it seems that the only thing you can do is to fall off without expostulation, and lo! the Falls as they appear in one of his pictures. Here, in a space not two feet wide, hanging halfway down the precipice, he or his brother John stand to paint. Above the suspension bridge, on a narrow strip of land, that juts into the rapids, I saw his brother at work this morning, on a very successful sketch of the great tumult before him. And wherever Niagara is beautiful and grand (and that is everywhere) the Frankensteins have transferred as much of that beauty and grandeur as paint can fix upon the canvas.

Goat Island is the constant scene of tender passages—a place of unlimited flirtation. In the presence of the great cataract, soul clings unconsciously to soul. You find yourself bellowing vain commonplaces of admiration to every one you meet, and you make acquaintance surprisingly easy. You can understand then how it happens, when young Jones strays upon the island with Miss Smith, (who is dressed in one of those bewitching suits of gray, and wears her beautiful hair in a broad roll under a jaunty Spanish hat,) how it happens, I say, that the arm of young Jones convulsively clasps the waist of Miss Smith at all thrilling points of view, and the little hands of Miss Smith grip the arm of young Jones. Happy people! straying under the trees, with the dancing shadows of the leaves upon you! Happy, indeed, if you could walk here forever, and not become Mr. and Mrs. Jones, and be old and fat.

So we said enviously, seeing the bliss of young Jones and Miss Smith, as they sat down in the shade, near the Hermit's Cascade, and drew near together, and made believe to read books, and knew nothing but love!

O Niagara! you are nothing; and O Hermit's Cascade! you are a mere turmoil of foam, and if the Hermit really bathed in you, (as that public character is said to have done,) then he had better have bathed safely, if not picturesquely, in a tub at home.

Niagara Falls, July 19, 1860.

Shall I add myself to the number of absurd people who have attempted to describe Niagara? . . .

It is hard to deny myself the luxury. One comes here with the best intentions of being sensible in the world, and then gives utterance to the most foolish incoherencies. I remember to have remarked to several people already, that the Falls are stupendous; that the spray is beautiful; that those rapids are fine, and the precipices frightful. But I certainly feel now that it was folly to do so—that I had better have said nothing, or said, with regard to the whole thing, that it was *nice*. That would have expressed the glory of the cataract—which lives in voices, lights, and immensities—as well as any other form of words. For the best that my art can do for Niagara is to *suggest* it. Whatever artist attempts more, is beat down helpless in the presence of its grandeur, and can only present the convulsions of his own ideas.

My first feeling on seeing the cataract, was that of vague disappointment. I had not figured anything greater, but something different,—or perhaps it did not impress me as I intended; for one always approaches the sublime with a pre-disposition to be glorified. It is the conventional habit of thought, which on a second glance at Niagara falls from you, and leaves you free to be affected naturally.

I have done the whole Cataract thoroughly, in my stay of two days—and I may speak by the card. When you first come (and let it be in the afternoon), take the car that descends from near Point Prospect to the river's edge, and then clamber over the rocks as close as you can to the foot of the American Falls, which is the point to experience your first sensations, and have your first rainbow, to realize Niagara, to unburden your mind of all old lumber of expectation, which you have stored away from pictures, and travels, and foolish poems—for all poems about Niagara are ridiculously inadequate.

From this point the Canada fall is almost hidden by heavy clouds of mist, that as you glance quickly at them, are full of delicate, fleeting dusks and purples, not seen with a steady look. Ascend now, and firmly, yet with that refined politeness natural to you, decline the hospitable offers of the numerous gentlemanly coach-men who desire the pleasure of taking you all around for an unnameable trifle, and cross the Suspension Bridge to Goat Island on foot.

Pass through the delicious little solitude in the heart of the Island, which the foot-path traverses, and emerge at Terrapin Tower, where half the civilized world has inscribed its names, in different styles of character, on the walls. If you find here the ubiquitous bore, who haunts even the presence of magnificence, frown upon him, and affect not to hear what he says. If you see an oldish gentleman, who clambers close to the brink of the precipice and looks over in the furious abyss, point the bore to him. If the bore should mildly expostulate with the oldish gentleman, and the oldish gentleman should reply that phrenologists have told him he can go anywhere without danger,—draw the conclusions of wisdom from the scene.

Then go up to the top of Terrapin Tower, and do your Horse Shoe Falls. When you sweep with one glance over the career of the tumultuous rapids, and leap (in your thoughts, gentle reader, in your thoughts,) down with that green translucent sea of falling water into the white and thundering gulf below—look hastily about, and if there is no one near, go crazy a little while to yourself. Then compose your countenance, and return to your hotel, pausing on the suspension bridge to gulp the American rapids.

. . .

There are so many things about Niagara that one thinks to say, that it fills with despair to contemplate the amount which must remain unsaid by the rapidest talkers. There are the smaller islands to mention, the far-seen picturesque shores, the black and frowning cliffs; there is the pretty little village at the Falls, with its bazaars of Indian work, and curiosity shops; there are the Indian women, who sit and embroider moccasins in the shady corners, and shatter your ideal of the Indian Maid; there are the studiable visitors in throngs from all parts of civilization; there is the hotel life, and its chance acquaintances and flirtations and fast livers. There is—An end for the present. To-morrow, I am off for Lake Ontario.

Henry James: "It Beats Michael Angelo"

(1843–1916)

It may have been Niagara Falls that made the novelist and travel writer Henry James, for a brief period of time, into an art critic. Well, Niagara, and William Dean Howells.

Shortly after becoming editor of the *Atlantic Monthly* on July 1, 1871, William Dean Howells asked his friend Henry James to contribute art reviews to the magazine. James had recently published a series of travel essays in *The Nation* on his impressions of American and Canadian scenery while on tours in the summer of 1870 and late summer and early fall of 1871. Howells's request is not surprising. James's travel writing paints pictures of places in words, perhaps most notably in his essay "Niagara."

Though "Niagara" was among his first travel essays, Henry James had been traveling since infancy. James was born into a cosmopolitan family. Over the course of his lifetime, he visited or stayed for extended periods in England, France, Switzerland, Germany, Belgium, Holland, Italy, and Canada. In America he lived in New York City, the place of his birth, as well as Boston, and would summer in Newport, Rhode Island and Saratoga Springs, New York. He lived the last decades of his life in England, becoming a naturalized British subject within a year after the start of the First World War. The many places he visited informed some of his most memorable fiction, including *Daisy Miller* (1879), *The Portrait of a Lady* (1881), and *The Ambassadors* (1903).

James had many experiences of the European picturesque by 1870, but it was on his native soil and neighboring Canada that his first-person experiences would take narrative form. Many more would follow. In his early collection of sketches, written between 1870 and 1871 on Quebec, Newport, Saratoga Springs, and Niagara Falls, the latter seems to stand out. As one literary critic put it: "It is only when the tourist confronts Niagara in the grandeur and desolation of its untamed magnificence that [James] abandons all caution and launches into one of the great bravura descriptive feats of his early prose."[9] James referred to his travel as an "aesthetic pilgrimage" and found that the Falls conformed to ideals of the picturesque, beauty, and the sublime.

From Toronto across Lake Ontario, James arrived in Niagara to stay on the American side in late September 1871. His hotel registration is dated September 25. (See figure 15.) (Coincidentally former president Millard Fillmore checked in to the hotel the next day.) James's article on his stay appeared in *The Nation* unsigned but was later republished in his travel essay collection fittingly titled *Portraits of Places* (1883). The essays are indeed "words of art."

Though the heyday of travel writing had passed, James's essays capture what the best travel narratives set out to do: create a picture in the reader's eye. James's essay moves from the picturesque—a framed view of

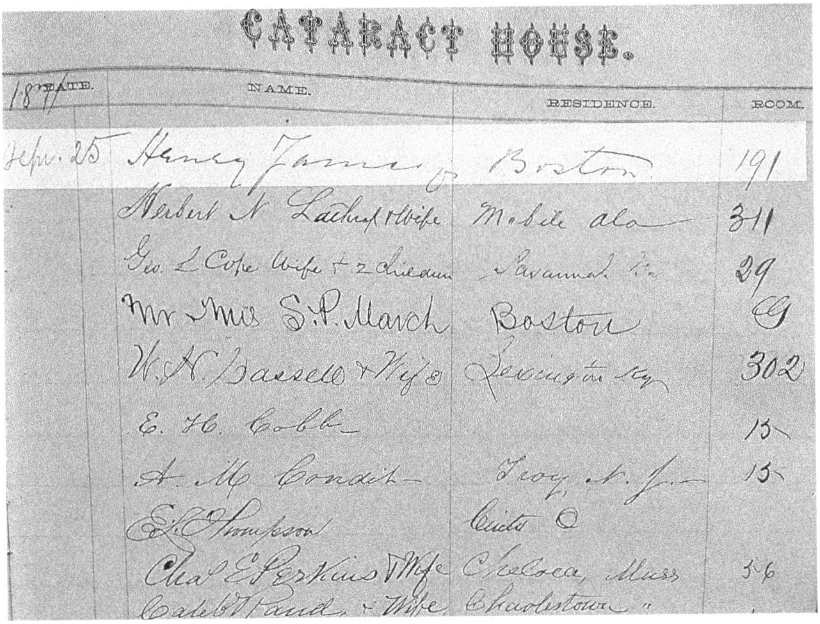

CATARACT HOUSE.

1871 DATE.	NAME.	RESIDENCE.	ROOM.
Sep. 25	Henry James	Boston	191
	Herbert N Latham & Wife	Mobile Ala	311
	Geo. L Cope Wife + 2 children	Savannah Ga	29
	Mr + Mrs S.P. March	Boston	G
	W. H. Bassell & Wife	Lexington Ky	302
	E. H. Cobb		15
	A. M. Condit	Troy N.Y.	15
	E. L. Thompson	Cinti O	
	Chas E Perkins & Wife	Chelsea, Mass	56
	Caleb H Rand & Wife	Charlestown "	

Figure 15. Henry James's Cataract House Hotel registration, September 25, 1871. Cataract House Register, September 23, 1871 to August 2, 1872. Niagara Falls Public Library.

the landscape—to an artistic and spiritual depiction of nature: "the passage of body to soul, of matter to spirit, of human to divine."

From "Niagara." *The Nation*. October 12–19, 1871.

My journey hitherward by a morning's sail from Toronto across Lake Ontario, seemed to me, as regards a certain dull vacuity in this episode of travel, a kind of calculated preparation for the uproar of Niagara—a pause or hush on the threshold of a great impression; and this, too, in spite of the reverent attention I was mindful to bestow on the first seen, in my experience, of the great lakes. It has the merit, from the shore, of producing a slight ambiguity of vision. It is the sea, and yet just not the sea. The huge expanse, the landless line of the horizon, suggest the ocean; while an indefinable shortness of pulse, a kind of freshwater gentleness of tone, seem to contradict the idea. What meets the eye is on the scale of the ocean, but you feel somehow that the lake is a thing of smaller spirit. . . .

At the mouth of the Niagara River, however, after a sail of three hours, scenery really begins, and very soon crowds upon you in force. The steamer puts into the narrow channel of the stream, and heads upward between high embankments. From this point, I think, you really enter into relations with Niagara. Little by little the elements become a picture, rich with the shadow of coming events. You have a foretaste of the great spectacle of colour which you enjoy at the Falls. The even cliffs of red-brown earth are crusted and spotted with autumnal orange and crimson, and, laden with this gorgeous decay, they plunge sheer into the deep-dyed green of the river.

As you proceed, the river begins to tell its tale at first in broken syllables of foam and flurry, and then, as it were, in rushing, flashing sentences and passionate ejaculations. Onwards from Lewiston, where you are transferred from the boat to the train, you see it from the edge of the American cliff, far beneath you, now superbly unnavigable. . . .

At the station pertaining to the railway suspension-bridge, you see in midair, beyond an interval of murky confusion produced at once by the farther bridge, the smoke of the trains, and the thickened atmosphere of the peopled bank, a huge far-flashing sheet which glares through the distance as a monstrous absorbent and irradiant of light. And here, in the interest of the picturesque, let me note that this obstructive bridge tends in a way to enhance the first glimpse of the cataract. Its long black span, falling dead along the shining brow of the Falls, seems shivered and smitten by their fierce effulgence, and trembles across the field of vision like some enormous mote in a light too brilliant. A moment later, as the train proceeds, you plunge into the village, and the cataract, save as a vague ground-tone to this trivial interlude, is, like so many other goals of aesthetic pilgrimage, temporarily postponed to the hotel. With this postponement comes, I think, an immediate decline of expectation; for there is every appearance that the spectacle you have come so far to see is to be choked in the horribly vulgar shops and booths and catchpenny artifices which have pushed and elbowed to within the very spray of the Falls, and ply their importunities in shrill competition with its thunder. You see a multitude of hotels and taverns and stores, glaring with white paint, bedizened with placards and advertisements, and decorated by groups of those gentlemen who flourish most rankly on the soil of New York and in the vicinage of hotels; who carry their hands in their pockets, wear their hats always and every way, and, although of a stationary habit, yet spurn the earth with their heels. A side-glimpse of the Falls, however, calls out your philosophy; you reflect that this may be regarded as one of those sordid foregrounds which Turner liked to use, and which may be effective as a foil; you hurry to where the roar grows louder, and, I was going to say, you escape from the village. In fact, however, you don't escape from it; it is constantly at your elbow, just to the right or the left of the line of contemplation. . . .

Though hereabouts so much is great, distances are small, and a ramble of two or three hours enables you to gaze hither and thither from a dozen standpoints. The one you are likely to choose first is that on the Canada cliff, a little way above the suspension-bridge. The great Fall faces you, enshrined in its own surging incense. The common feeling just here, I believe, is one of disappointment at its want of height; the whole thing appears to many people somewhat smaller than its fame. My own sense, I confess, was absolutely gratified from the first; and, indeed, I was not struck with anything being tall or short, but with everything being perfect. You are, moreover, at some distance, and you feel that with the lessening interval you will not be cheated of your chance to be dizzied with mere dimensions. Already you see the world-famous green, baffling painters, baffling poets, shining on the lip of the precipice; the more so, of course, for the clouds of silver and snow into which it speedily resolves itself. The whole picture before you is admirably simple. The Horseshoe glares and boils and smokes from the centre to the right, drumming itself into powder and thunder; in the centre the dark pedestal of Goat Island divides the double flood; to the left booms in vaporous dimness the minor battery of the American Fall; while on a level with the eye, above the still crest of either cataract, appear the white faces of the hithermost rapids. The circle of weltering froth at the base of the Horseshoe, emerging from the dead white vapours—absolute white, as moonless midnight is absolute black—which muffle impenetrably the crash of the river upon the lower bed, melts slowly into the darker shades of green. . . .

The perfect taste of it is the great characteristic. It is not in the least monstrous; it is thoroughly artistic and, as the phrase is, thought out. In the matter of line it beats Michael Angelo. One may seem at first to say the least, but the careful observer will admit that one says the most, in saying that it *pleases*—pleases even a spectator who was not ashamed to write the other day that he didn't care for cataracts. . . .

If the line of beauty had vanished from the earth elsewhere, it would survive on the brow of Niagara. It is impossible to insist too strongly on the grace of the thing, as seen from the Canada cliff. The genius who invented it was certainly the first author of the idea that order, proportion and symmetry are the conditions of perfect beauty. He applied his faith among the watching and listening forests, long before the Greeks proclaimed theirs in the measurements of the Parthenon. Even the roll of the white batteries at the base seems fixed and poised and ordered, and in the vague middle zone of difference between the flood as it falls and the mist as it rises you imagine a mystical meaning—the passage of body to soul, of matter to spirit, of human to divine.

Chapter 8

War, and Peace

*T*hough the Niagara frontier has a long history of conflict and war, it has a longer history of peace. Both stories can be found in the Constitution of the Haudenosaunee (Iroquois) Confederacy, well before Europeans arrived in the region.[1] The Haudenosaunee Confederacy began in what is now central and western New York State as a league of Five Nations—Mohawk, Oneida, Onondaga, Cayuga, and Seneca. The Tuscarora, displaced to the region in the early eighteenth century, were invited to make up the now Six Nations of the Haudenosaunee.[2]

The constitution of the Haudenosaunee, the "Great Binding Law" or Great Law of Peace, created community out of independent nations, its democratic principles becoming a model for the US Constitution. Recorded in wampum[3] and later written in English by the twentieth-century historian, archaeologist, and writer of Iroquois descent, Arthur Caswell Parker, the *Constitution* begins with the planting of the Tree of the Great Peace, whose "roots have spread out . . . one to the north, one to the east, one to the south and one to the west. The name of these roots is The Great White Roots and their nature is Peace and Strength."[4] A document of law and of peaceful alliance between nations, however, the constitution, like all such, also had provision for war.

Memories and markers of war remain in the Niagara River region: seventeenth-century conflicts during the height of the fur trade; eighteenth- and early-nineteenth-century settler conflicts for colonial territory; twentieth-century munitions and antimissile batteries; and twenty-first-century remnants of nuclear waste from "The Manhattan Project," the making of the atomic bomb.

In his 2007 posthumously published collection *Big Medicine from Six Nations*, Tuscarora writer Ted Williams asked, "So we have the Great Law of the Great Peace, but do we have it at a level to live it?"[5] It is a sentiment that may have been shared by writers who went to the Falls in times of war. Traveling during the Civil War, Anthony Trollope found the Falls to be a place of peace. For Rupert Brooke, the Falls were a place of contemplation in the face of rising international tension, the impending First World War of the twentieth century.

Anthony Trollope: The Civil War

(1815–1882)

When the British novelist Anthony Trollope came to the United States in 1861 with the intent of writing a travel book, he admits that he, "should not purposely have chosen this period either for my book or my visit." Nevertheless, here, in this moment, he finds that he must "write of the war, of the causes which have led to it, and of its probable termination." The war features heavily in his travel book—with the exception, that is, of his visit to Niagara Falls.

After nearly half a year of traveling to British colonies on duties associated with his management position in the post office, Anthony Trollope embarked on a short Northern Tour in America in mid-June 1859. From New York City he made his way north via the Hudson River to Albany. Claiming "there is nothing to be seen at Albany," he traveled the night train on the New York Central Railway to Niagara Falls. Mistakenly taking the train to the Niagara Falls station rather than crossing at Suspension Bridge station, Trollope had to pay five dollars to get from the American to the Canadian side—a rather pricey amount considering the train ticket from Albany to Niagara cost him only six dollars. "So much for Niagara," he soon concludes. Trollope completed his abbreviated tour traveling by steamboat across Lake Ontario to Montreal, finding the lake "uninteresting, being altogether too large for scenery, and too foggy for sight-seeing if there were anything to see."[6] Despite his blasé attitude, the experiences he records of Niagara Falls during this initial visit appear again in his subsequent travel book, *North America* (1862).

By October 1861, Trollope was bound for America again. His intention was to investigate the causes of and solutions to the American Civil War, now in its first full year. The war made it difficult to travel to Southern states, but Trollope observed the political landscape, discussed secession with abolitionists, camped with army officers near the Confederate front, and visited the slave state of Kentucky. Despite this "research," Trollope minimized the plight of slaves, with only one farm as his evidence of living conditions, and he argued that immediate abolition would not work, as even the North was unprepared for true equality. But he saw slavery as an evil, belittling to all, and argued that a war to fight against it was worth the division it wrought. The North, he predicted, would win.

Despite his frequent commentary on the war throughout his lengthy two-volume travel book, *North America*, Trollope's discussion of the Falls remains an exception. It does not engage in war discourse. His interest here is purely the experience of the tourist. From Toronto, Trollope traveled to Niagara likely aboard a steamboat, "reentering the States at Lewiston, in New York." Again writing with the authority of a travel guide, he directs his readers to get the most value for their time and money. Ultimately, however, Trollope advises that the best path is the one that leads to a silencing of the outside world.

In an 1862 prepublication review of *North America*, a writer for the *Evening Post* compares the novelist son to his mother's earlier travel narrative.[7] In "A Chip Off the Old Block," the reviewer writes: "Mrs. Frances Trollope, some thirty years ago, wrote a spicy and spiteful book on America." This book, *Domestic Manners of Americans* (1832), based on her stay in the US from 1827 to 1830, was a best seller, despite its unpopularity among Americans. Anthony Trollope's publication fared better, if not in sales, then in public opinion. With some exceptions, the son's is the more fair book, the reviewer concludes, not least for its Niagara reflections, in which Trollope finds peace in the context of war.

From *North America* (New York:
Harper and Brothers Publishers, 1862)

Chapter VII: Niagara

Of all the sights on this earth of ours which tourists travel to see—at least of all those which I have seen—I am inclined to give the palm to the Falls of Niagara. In the catalogue of such sights I intend to include all buildings, pictures, statues, and wonders of art made by men's hands, and also all beauties of nature prepared by the Creator for the delight of his creatures. . . .

. . . How many cataracts does the habitual tourist visit at which the waters fail him! But at Niagara the waters never fail. There it thunders over its ledge in a volume that never ceases and is never diminished—as it has done from times previous to the life of man, and as it will do till tens of thousands of years shall see the rocky bed of the river worn away back to the upper lake.

. . . the Clifton House was closed for the season when I was last there, and on that account we went to the Cataract House, in the town on the other side. I now think that I should set up my staff on the American side, if I went again. My advice on the subject to any party starting for Niagara would depend upon their habits or on their nationality. I would send Americans to the Canadian side, because they dislike walking; but English people I would locate on the American side, seeing that they are generally accustomed to the frequent use of their own legs. The two sides are not very easily approached one from the other. Immediately below the falls there is a ferry, which may be traversed at the expense of a shilling; but the labor of getting up and down from the ferry is considerable, and the passage becomes wearisome. There is also a bridge; but it is two miles down the river, making a walk or drive of four miles necessary, and the toll for passing is four shillings, or a dollar, in a carriage, and one shilling on foot. As the greater variety of prospect can be had on the American side, as the island between the two falls is approachable from the American side and not from the Canadian, and as it is in this island that visitors will best love to linger, and learn to measure in their minds the vast triumph of waters before them, I recommend such of my readers as can trust a little—it need be but a little—to their own legs to select their hotel at Niagara Falls town. . . .

Go down to the end of that wooden bridge, seat yourself on the rail, and there sit till all the outer world is lost to you. There is no grander spot about Niagara than this. The waters are absolutely around you. If you have that power of eye-control which is so necessary to the full enjoyment of scenery, you will see nothing but the water. You will certainly hear nothing else; and the sound, I beg you to remember, is not an ear-cracking, agonizing crash and clang of noises, but is melodious and soft withal, though loud as thunder. It fills your ears, and, as it were, envelops them, but at the same time you can speak to your neighbor without an effort. But at this place, and in these moments, the less of speaking, I should say, the better. There is no grander spot than this. Here, seated on the rail of the bridge, you will not see the whole depth of the fall. . . .

To realize Niagara, you must sit there till you see nothing else than that which you have come to see. You will hear nothing else, and think of nothing else. At length you will be at one with the tumbling river before you. You will find yourself among the waters as though you belonged to them. The cool, liquid green will run through your veins, and the voice of the cataract will be the expression of your own heart. You will fall as the bright waters fall, rushing down into your new world with no hesitation and with no dismay; and you will rise again as the spray rises, bright, beautiful, and pure. Then you will flow away in your course to the uncompassed, distant, and eternal ocean.

When this state has been reached and has passed away, you may get off your rail and mount the tower. I do not quite approve of that tower, seeing that it has about it a gingerbread air, and reminds one of those well-arranged scenes of romance in which one is told that on the left you turn to the lady's bower, price sixpence; and on the right ascend to the knight's bed, price sixpence more, with a view of the hermit's tomb thrown in. But nevertheless the tower is worth mounting, and no money is charged for the use of it. It is not very high, and there is a balcony at the top on which some half dozen persons may stand at ease. Here the mystery is lost, but the whole fall is seen. . . .

But we are still on the tower; and here I must declare that though I forgive the tower, I cannot forgive the horrid obelisk which has latterly been built opposite to it, on the Canadian side, up above the fall; built apparently—for I did not go to it—with some camera-obscura intention for which the projector deserves to be put in Coventry by all good Christian men and women. At such a place as Niagara tasteless buildings, run up in wrong places with a view to money making, are perhaps necessary evils. It may be that they are not evils at all; that they give more pleasure than pain, seeing that they tend to the enjoyment of the multitude. But there are edifices of this description which cry aloud to the gods by the force of their own ugliness and malposition. As to such, it may be said that there should somewhere exist a power capable of crushing them in their birth. This new obelisk, or picture-building at Niagara, is one of such. . . .

The readiest way across to Canada is by the ferry; and on the American side this is very pleasantly done. You go into a little house, pay twenty cents, take a seat on a wooden car of wonderful shape, and on the touch of a spring find yourself traveling down an inclined plane of terrible declivity, and at a very fast rate. You catch a glance of the river below you, and recognize the fact that if the rope by which you are held should break, you would go down at a very fast rate indeed, and find your final resting-place in the river. As I have gone down some dozen times, and have come to no such grief, I will not presume that you will be less lucky. Below there is a boat generally ready. If it be not there, the place is not chosen amiss for a rest of ten minutes, for the lesser fall is close at hand, and the larger one is in full view. . . .

Having mounted the hill on the Canada side you will walk on towards the falls. . . . Close to the cataract, exactly at the spot from whence in former days the Table Rock used to project from the land over the boiling caldron below, there is now a shaft down which you will descend to the level of the river, and pass between the rock and the torrent. . . .

In the spot to which I allude the visitor stands on a broad, safe path, made of shingles, between the rock over which the water rushes and the rushing water. He will go in so far that the spray, rising back from the bed of the torrent, does not incommode him. With this exception, the farther he can go in the better; but circumstances will clearly show him the spot to which he should advance. Unless the water be driven in by a very strong wind, five yards make the difference between a comparatively dry coat and an absolutely wet one. And then let him stand with his back to the entrance, thus hiding the last glimmer of the expiring day. So standing, he will look up among the falling waters, or down into the deep, misty pit, from which they re-ascend in almost as palpable a bulk. The rock will be at his right hand, high and hard, and dark and straight, like the wall of some huge cavern, such as children enter in their dreams. For the first five minutes he will be looking but at the waters of a cataract—at the waters, indeed, of such a cataract as we know no other, and at their interior curves which elsewhere we cannot see. But by-and-by all this will change. He will no longer be on a shingly path beneath a waterfall; but that feeling of a cavern wall will grow upon him, of a cavern deep, below roaring seas, in which the waves are there, though they do not enter in upon him; or rather, not the waves, but the very bowels of the ocean. He will feel as though the floods surrounded him, coming and going with their wild sounds, and he will hardly recognize that though among them he is not in them. And they, as they fall with a continual roar, not hurting the ear, but musical withal, will seem to move as the vast ocean waters may perhaps move in their internal currents. He will lose the sense of one continued descent, and think that they are passing round him in their appointed courses. The broken spray that rises from the depths below, rises so strongly, so palpably, so rapidly that the motion in every direction will seem equal. And, as he looks on, strange colors will show themselves through the mist; the shades of gray will become green or blue, with ever and anon a flash of white; and then, when some gust of wind blows in with greater violence, the sea-girt cavern will become all dark and black. Oh, my friend, let there be no one there to speak to thee then; no, not even a brother. As you stand there speak only to the waters.

Rupert Brooke: "The Great War"

(1887–1915)

In his travel essay "Niagara Falls," written a year before the outbreak of the First World War (1914–1918), Rupert Brooke wrote of the significance of place in defining one's experience. It is a sentiment he was remembered for from his popular poem "The Soldier," written in the early months of the war as young British men fought and died in France.

> "If I should die, think only this of me:
> That there's some corner of a foreign field
> That is for ever England."

So begins Rupert Brooke's 1914 sonnet "The Soldier." The poem romanticized the soldier as a symbol of national pride on foreign soil. Brooke had volunteered for war, receiving a commission in the British Royal Navy, and by October 1914 was sent to Antwerp, Belgium, where he encountered shelling during the city's siege and fall. "The Soldier" reflects on sacrifice, compelling those back home to remember the fallen. Written early in the war, the sonnet was famously read at St. Paul's Cathedral on Easter, April 4, 1915, as a model of patriotism, an attitude that subsequent realist British war poets, such as Siegfried Sassoon, Wilfred Owen, and Isaac Rosenberg, and the Canadian poet and physician John McCrae,[8] would reject amid the devastating casualties and brutalities of modern warfare.

Brooke died on April 23, 1915, from a blood infection on board a ship to Gallipoli. Winston Churchill, then First Lord of the Admiralty, whom Brooke knew through a mutual friend, wrote of the soldier-poet in the London *Times*:

> A voice had become audible, a note had been struck, more true, more thrilling, more able to do justice to the nobility of our youth in arms engaged in this present war, than any other more able to express their thoughts of self-surrender, and with a power to carry comfort to those who watch them so intently from afar. The voice has been swiftly stilled. Only the echoes and the memory remain; but they will linger.[9]

The "for ever England" of Brooke's poem was itself an echo of an earlier sentiment sounded in his travel narrative on Niagara Falls, which also connected experience to the landscape. In May 1913, Brooke set sail for North America and then on to Pacific islands. After touring sites like New York, Boston, and Quebec, he crossed Lake Ontario to Toronto and then traveled to Niagara Falls, Canada, writing travel letters to the *Westminster Gazette* about his experiences. These pieces were collected after his death and published as *Letters from America* (1916). The collection closed with another essay of Brooke's, "An Unusual Young Man," a reflection on first hearing England was at war.

Though criticism of Brooke's war poems was often that they were sentimental, his travel writing was realistic, if not at times ironic. From Toronto, Brooke sent newspaper clippings to his longtime friend, James Strachey,[10] noting dryly, "how frightfully life's everywhere the same." And though he claims to approach the natural wonder of the Falls as a respite from "human nature," his essay ranks with Margaret Fuller, Charles Dickens, and Mark Twain as among the harsher critiques of the tourist traps and those associated with them, who he refers to as "touts"—sellers and schemers who solicit the weary tourist and sully the view. Only in juxtaposition to such spectacle do the meaning and majesty of the Falls come into focus. Amid the sublime, Brooke notes, one transcends humanity's ordinary concerns and engages higher truths.

But to seek pattern and stability in the Falls, as in life, is only to realize that all is ultimately change and chaos. Well aware, like others, of the tenuous political climate in Europe in 1913, Brooke reads in the Falls an image eerily prescient of the coming war—it is symbolic of ruin for individual and nation alike. As in "The Soldier," how one chooses to meet this end is meaningful.

From "Niagara Falls," *Letters from America* (1916)

. . . It is very restful to give up all effort at observing human nature and drawing social and political deductions from trifles, and to let oneself relapse into wide-mouthed worship of the wonders of nature. And this is very easy at Niagara. Niagara means nothing. It is not leading anywhere. It does not result from anything. It throws no light on the effects of Protection, nor on the Facility for Divorce in America, nor on Corruption in Public Life, nor on Canadian character, nor even on the Navy Bill. It is merely a great deal of water falling over some cliffs. But it is very remarkably that. The human race, apt as a child to destroy what it admires, has done its best to surround the Falls with every distraction, incongruity, and vulgarity. Hotels, power-houses, bridges, trams, picture post-cards, sham legends, stalls, booths, rifle-galleries, and side-shows frame them about. And there are Touts. Niagara is the central home and breeding-place for all the touts of earth. There are touts insinuating, and touts raucous, greasy touts, brazen touts, and upper-class, refined, gentlemanly, take-you-by-the-arm touts; touts who intimidate and touts who wheedle; professionals, amateurs, and dilettanti, male and female; touts who would photograph you with your arm round a young lady against a faked background of the sublimest cataract, touts who would bully you into cars, char-a-bancs, elevators, or tunnels, or deceive you into a carriage and pair, touts who would sell you picture postcards, moccasins, sham Indian beadwork, blankets, tee-pees, and crockery; and touts, finally, who have no apparent object in the world, but just purely, simply, merely, incessantly, indefatigably, and ineffugibly[11]—to tout. And in the midst of all this, overwhelming it all, are the Falls. He who sees them instantly forgets humanity. They are not very high, but they are overpowering. . . .

Half a mile or so above the Falls, on either side, the water of the great stream begins to run more swiftly and in confusion. It descends with ever-growing speed. It begins chattering and leaping, breaking into a thousand ripples, throwing up joyful fingers of spray. Sometimes it is divided by islands and rocks, sometimes the eye can see nothing but a waste of laughing, springing, foamy waves, turning, crossing, even seeming to stand for an instant erect, but always borne impetuously forward like a crowd of triumphant feasters. Sit close down by it, and you see a fragment of the torrent against the sky, mottled, steely, and foaming, leaping onward in far-flung criss-cross strands of water. Perpetually the eye is on the point of descrying a pattern in this weaving, and perpetually it is cheated by change. In one place part of the flood plunges over a ledge a few feet high and a quarter of a mile or so long, in a uniform and stable curve. It gives an impression of almost military concerted movement, grown suddenly out of confusion. . . .

But there they change. As they turn to the sheer descent, the white and blue and slate-colour, in the heart of the Canadian Falls at least, blend and deepen to a rich, wonderful, luminous green. On the edge of disaster the river seems to gather herself, to pause, to lift a head noble in ruin, and then, with a slow grandeur, to plunge into the eternal thunder and white chaos below. . . .

And always there are the rainbows. If you come suddenly upon the Falls from above, a great double rainbow, very vivid, spanning the extent of spray from top to bottom, is the first thing you see. If you wander along the cliff opposite, a bow springs into being in the American Falls, accompanies you courteously on your walk, dwindles and dies as the mist ends, and awakens again as you reach the Canadian tumult. And the bold traveler who attempts the trip under the American Falls sees, when he dare open his eyes to anything, tiny baby rainbows, some four or five yards in span, leaping from rock to rock among the foam, and gambolling beside him, barely out of hand's reach, as he goes. One I saw in that place was a complete circle, such as I have never seen before, and so near that I could put my foot on it. It is a terrifying journey, beneath and behind the Falls. The senses are battered and bewildered by the thunder of the water and the assault of wind and spray; or rather, the sound is not of falling water, but merely of falling; a noise of unspecified ruin. So, if you are close behind the endless clamour, the sight cannot recognise liquid in the masses that hurl past. You are dimly and pitifully aware that sheets of light and darkness are falling in great curves in front of you. Dull omnipresent foam washes the face. Farther away, in the roar and hissing, clouds of spray seem literally to slide down some invisible plane of air. . . .

A man's life is of many flashing moments, and yet one stream; a nation's flows through all its citizens, and yet is more than they. In such places, one is aware, with an almost insupportable and yet comforting certitude, that both men and nations are hurried onwards to their ruin or ending as inevitably as this dark flood. Some go down to it unreluctant, and meet it, like the river, not without nobility. And as incessant, as inevitable, and as unavailing as the spray that hangs over the Falls, is the white cloud of human crying. . . . With some such thoughts does the platitudinous heart win from the confusion and thunder of Niagara a peace that the quietest plains or most stable hills can never give.

Chapter 9

Case Closed?

*T*hough the Falls are arguably a site of contemplation, wonder, and awe, several writers also make mention of the mesmerizing and disorienting nature of the waterfall. Others write of its ability to "swallow" all within its power. From battles to daredevilry to suicides to corruption, it is fair to say that Niagara Falls is a place of mystery, intrigue, and unanswered questions.

Of the many writers and stories in this book, questions remain: Was it Charles Dickens who signed a poem "Boz" in the *Table Rock Album*, despite his own judgment of the album's debased expressions? In a later rewrite for *The Niagara Book* of his 1860 visit to the Falls, William Dean Howells told of seeing a body on the rocks below when he crept to the brink of Horseshoe Falls. Was it trauma that kept him from writing about it for over thirty years? What happened to the guest registry books of hotels that did not burn down but are missing from collections in local libraries and historical societies? How many manuscripts are in private hands that might someday, like the Whirlpools Rapids, churn up definitive proof of, say, James Fenimore Cooper's supposed visit to the region in 1821?

Occasionally, writers who visited Niagara Falls, such as Cooper, Jack London, and Sir Arthur Conan Doyle, found themselves less the authors of their own lives than characters facing conflict—in court cases, in mysteries, and in historical debates. Their experiences added to their own legendary fame, but they also contribute to the literary legends of the region. And, their experiences illustrate, once again, truth can prove stranger than fiction.

James Fenimore Cooper: Historical Fictions

(1789–1851)

The closing chapter of James Fenimore Cooper's 1821 novel The Spy *finds its protagonist at Niagara Falls, a fictional conclusion that has been taken as historical fact of the author's presence in the region that year. But like other Cooper connections to the Falls, this one is not without dispute.*

Among the most cited stories along the Niagara Frontier is that of famed early American author James Fenimore Cooper, a writer of both fiction, such as his well-known novel *The Last of the Mohicans* (1826), and of nonfiction, such as *History of the Navy of the United States* (1839). Though he gained popularity for his historical fiction, Cooper has long been the subject of much historical dispute. Legend has it that Cooper's 1821 novel *The Spy: A Tale of Neutral Ground*, credited with the first mention of a drink called a "cocktail," was written in Lewiston, New York, just north of Niagara Falls, where Cooper visited that year "for an extended stay" to write his novel. Historians of the cocktail disagree with the drink's origin. If claims to Cooper's novel as the first use of "cocktail" can be questioned, what other details of the legend might be up for debate?

Though *The Spy* ends at Niagara Falls during the War of 1812, its plot unfolds during the Revolutionary War. Set primarily in Westchester County, New York, the novel follows the story of Harvey Birch, a character fictionalized as the first American spy but who posed as a British spy during the Revolutionary War. Birch was believed to be a traitor and so disappeared from the public eye. The end of the novel finds Birch first at the Falls and then crossing the Niagara River when he is wounded in a War of 1812 battle. Upon his death, the truth of his service to America in the earlier war is finally recovered.

The character of interest to Lewiston legend, however, is a tavern owner in the novel at "the village of the Four Corners," Elizabeth Flanagan (aka Betty) who sells provisions to soldiers. Betty Flanagan is a colorful character who drinks too much and uses indecent language, but she is nevertheless revered for her "unbounded love of her adopted country." Flanagan is argued to be based on Lewiston resident Catherine "Kitty"

Hustler, who with her husband Thomas Hustler, ran a tavern in Lewiston prior to and during the War of 1812. In Cooper's novel, "Betty" is credited with "inventing" the cocktail.

It is possible that Cooper met the Hustlers when he came to the Niagara region from 1809 to 1811, while in the navy, though documentation on such a meeting is lacking. What historians *have* been able to document, however, is that the use of the term *cocktail* emerged prior to Cooper's 1821 use of it. The first use of the word found in American papers is this unsurprising 1806 definition: "a stimulating liquor, composed of spirits of any kind, sugar, water, and bitters." More interesting is the same article's reference to cocktail to describe a political candidate accused of buying votes with booze.[1] Nevertheless, the focus on the case of the cocktail has obscured other Cooper connections to Niagara.

Documentation does exist for three very different trips Cooper made to the Niagara Frontier. In one of his historical essays, Cooper recounts an 1809 journey with the navy in which he spared soldiers from hunger after their provisions had run out when he "accidentally came across a hedge-hog, which he killed with the sword of a cane."[2] Hedgehogs are not native to North America, and it's more likely, as biographer Wayne Franklin notes, that Cooper came upon a porcupine. "On this animal, all hands supped," Cooper writes; "and very good eating it proved to be." The narrative device of the hero, though useful in any novel, appears to aid Cooper's nonfiction as well.

In another of his texts on the navy, Cooper's historical facts were publicly questioned in his own day. One such dispute was his portrayal of Captain Oliver Hazard Perry and his command of the ship the *Niagara* during the Battle of Lake Erie (1813). Critics argued that Cooper's *History of the Navy of the United States of America* diminished Perry's victory in the War of 1812 battle. At dispute were the actions of the original captain of the *Niagara*, Captain Jesse D. Elliott, who, it was thought, had failed to move his ship in quickly enough to support Perry's ship, the *Lawrence*, which had endured heavy artillery from the British. Though Elliott's actions later came into question, even by Perry himself, Cooper's *History* did not reflect that change. Reviewers publicly attacked Cooper for his portrayal of the heroism of both Perry *and* Elliott. Not for the first or last time during his career, Cooper brought libel suits against the negative reviewers and their publishers. On this occasion, the court decided in his favor.

Cooper would be less successful in the outcomes of other court cases, however, such as that concerning business dealings in Michigan beginning in 1847, the year of his next documented visit to the Niagara region.[3] Just under a decade prior, Cooper had invested money in land speculations near Chicago, Illinois, during the Midwest "land boom." When he decided to sell the property so he could fund publishing travel books, the speculator he had invested in could not repay him in cash but offered as security a mortgage and bank notes the man had backed for land in Michigan. With the economic recession in 1837, however, Cooper was unable to recover all of his losses. By the mid-1840s, he brought suits against the debtors, necessitating his 1847 trip and several others between then and 1850.

Similar to his character in *The Spy*, Cooper perhaps saw himself as the moral hero of unjust situations. He was defamed in American newspapers and a victim of unfair business practices. Passing through the Niagara region in 1847, Cooper found comfort in stopping off at the Falls, to see "its surpassing beauty."

It was not until 1850 that Cooper "did the falls effectually" while on tour with his wife Susan and daughter Charlotte. On this visit, he could finally be free of controversy, once, that is, he assessed the danger of the *Maid of the Mist*:

> I do not think there is any danger, though there is a devil of a roaring, nor do I think the boat could be forced against the surges under the fall. I suppose we must have been thirty fathoms from the falling sheet, except as we came up in the eddy under Goat Island, where we must have been within half that distance. The boat comes up from the Suspension Bridge, a distance of two miles, and the scenery is beautiful. Table Rock, or what is left of it, is still the best place to see the Falls, but the passage in the boat is the most exciting and agreeable. My wife was delighted, and so far from being afraid, she scampered around the boat with the rest, like a girl of sixteen.[4]

Though others of Cooper's connections to the Niagara region are not without their questions and doubts, here there can be little dispute. Neither historical fact nor fiction are adequate to convey the experience of passing beneath the Falls.

Sir Arthur Conan Doyle: Sherlock and Spiritualism

(1859–1930)

> *The* Niagara Falls Gazette *asked Arthur Conan Doyle on his first visit to Niagara Falls on November 26, 1894, to give "his impression of this great natural curiosity." Conan Doyle remarked on "Its immensity." The* Gazette *used the author's reply as a headline.*[5] *It paled in comparison, however, to headlines that circulated during Conan Doyle's second visit to the region in May 1922.*

Sir Arthur Conan Doyle (knighted in 1902) arrived in Buffalo, New York on May 11, 1922, where he was scheduled to give a lecture. His wife and children made the long trip from England with him, but left him in Buffalo to do his work. They set out by train for Niagara Falls, New York, where Conan Doyle planned to meet up with them the next day. After a fifty-minute ride on that late spring evening, they were expected to arrive safely at Prospect House on the American side of the Falls. Like a page out of one of his Sherlock Holmes mysteries, however, Sir Arthur Conan Doyle's family went missing, never arriving at their destination. (See figure 16.)

It was a tale Conan Doyle seemed himself to have written. As he put it later that year in his travel narrative, *Our American Adventure* (1923): "It seemed to me as if a small mystery tale which I once wrote, where a certain train started from one junction and never arrived at the next one, never being heard of again, had actually come back upon me."

Figure 16. "Lady Conan Doyle 'Lost' Six Hours," *Buffalo Courier*, April 27, 1922, to May 21, 1922, NY 96, Buffalo 93-31534, Box 318. New York State Library.

Conan Doyle wanted to surprise his family with a phone call after finishing his lecture, but the Prospect House had no evidence of their arrival. With his secretary and his manager, Conan Doyle began to call other local hotels, but none had registered his family. By midnight, just as he was about to leave Buffalo to search Niagara Falls himself, Conan Doyle received the longed-for call: his family was safely lodged at the Lafayette Hotel on the Canadian side of the Falls. (See figures 17 and 18.)

The case of the missing family was not the only reason Conan Doyle made the news in 1922, however. Though the creator of Sherlock Holmes was greeted with fanfare on his first American lecture tour in 1894, by the time of his 1922 American adventure, attention had not abated, but it

THE EVENING WORLD,

Even "Sherlock Holmes" Fails To Find Lost Wife and Children

Mystery of Niagara Falls, N. Y., or Canadian City, Balks Conan Doyle, Seeking Family.

BUFFALO, N. Y., May 1.—All the deductive powers with which he endowed Sherlock Holmes, most famous detective of fiction, were employed by Sir Arthur Conan Doyle to find his wife and children, lost to him for six hours late last night.

The methods of Sherlock Holmes, however, proved not speedy enough for the distinguished spiritualist-lecturer, and the long-distance telephone was finally brought into play, with the result that Lady Conan Doyle and her children were located at a Niagara Falls, Ontario, hotel.

Lady Conan Doyle and the children left Buffalo for Niagara Falls last evening. Sir Arthur decided to join them. The hotel where reservations had been made had not heard of them. All the hotels in Niagara Falls, N. Y., were reached, without result. Then the creator of Sherlock Holmes, decidedly disturbed, got busy in earnest. He cross-examined the porter who had handled Lady Conan Doyle's baggage and the conductor of the train on which they had departed. Finally, as Sir Arthur was about to start out, with his secretary in the role of Dr. Watson, on a personal search of Niagara Falls, N. Y., word came from the Canadian Niagara Falls that the rest of the Doyles were safe there.

Figure 17. "Even 'Sherlock Holmes' Fails to Find Lost Wife and Children," *Evening World*, May 12, 1922. Wall Street Final Edition, p. 14, img. 14. Image provided by the New York Public Library, Astor, Lenox, and Tilden Foundation. Chronicling America: Historic American Newspapers, Library of Congress.

Figure 18. "Wife of Author Rests Quietly at Niagara Falls, Ont., Hotel," *Buffalo Courier*, April 27, 1922, to May 21, 1922, NY 96, Buffalo 93-31534, Box 318. New York State Library.

took a turn for the worse. Conan Doyle had become the subject of much debate. His lecture tour was no longer on literature but on spiritualism, and his readership was skeptical.

Spiritualism as a religious movement began in the mid-nineteenth century, based in the idea that a person's immaterial spirit continued in the afterlife and communicated through mediums to guide the living. The movement got its modern American start in Hydesville, New York, at the home of the Fox sisters, Margaret and Kate, who reportedly communed with a murdered salesman through knockings and rappings. Other means of accessing spirits of the deceased included séances, automatic writing, and psychic readings.

Conan Doyle believed in the ability to communicate with the spirits of the dead. Who could blame him? It was a conviction that escalated with the loss of his son, his brother, two nephews, and two brothers-in-law in "The Great War."[6] His published works on spiritualism's tenets, and his advocacy of its mainstream acceptance, garnered him a great deal of public criticism, however. His lectures in America were no exception.

The Friday, June 23, edition of the *Niagara Falls Gazette*, for example, ran a syndicated column from Philadelphia, Pennsylvania, with the headline: "Theories of Conan Doyle are Refuted by Famous Scholar." The article contained the subtitle "Spiritism [sic] is only Revamped Necromancy, Declares Dr. Paul L. S. Johnson," a leading Biblical scholar of the period. Johnson equates "spiritism" with ancient heathenism. He ridicules Doyle who, despite his "unusually full and level head and, better still, a good kind heart," "has only one empty lobe in his brains." Using Doyle's other writing successes against him, Johnson argues that the creator of Sherlock Holmes "has failed completely as a detective." Johnson does not refute the very idea of communicating with spirits. Rather, his concern is that the spirits communicated with are "the devil's underlings," "fallen angels—devils or demons—who impersonate the dead."

The *Lockport Union-Sun and Journal*, in Lockport, New York, also ran a syndicated article, this one from London, titled "Life in Hereafter Is Simply Living on Thinks Conan Doyle,"[7] in which the journalist tries to "poke holes" in Conan Doyle's theory. He asks what would become of Conan Doyle if the journalist shot him six times at that very moment. Conan Doyle responds, incredulous (not, notably, to the violent proposition of someone shooting him but to the belief in the supposed absoluteness of death posed by the question): "can anyone in his right senses believe that a little piece of lead is actually capable of destroying a mind and an intelligence which, God-given, has been in process of maturation through ancestors for aeons and aeons?" This mind and intelligence, Conan Doyle goes on to explain, has the potential to realize more "enlightened spheres where it has work to perform"—possibly that knowledge and experience gained in life passes on to those still living.

Though critical of Conan Doyle, each of these articles took seriously their tasks of reviewing his work, unlike the *Niagara Falls Gazette* of Wednesday, September 27, 1922, which had some fun on the heels of Conan Doyle's visit to the Falls—at Doyle's expense. Here, the afterlife of the literary legend's visit provides fodder for another mystery: "Atmospheric

Changes Direct Ghosts on the Upper Bridge," which mentions the recent visit of Sir and Mrs. Conan Doyle.

Ultimately, it is not clear whether the tale of Conan Doyle's missing family was staged for the papers, in a preemptive attempt to remind audiences that he was still the creator of the much-loved detective Sherlock, rather than solely a spiritualist. That the resolution of the case also made use of the telephone was likely not coincidental. Conan Doyle delivered his Buffalo lecture at the opening of "one of the most powerful radio broadcasting stations," the new WGR station, owned and operated by the Federal Telegraph and Telephone Company. It may, after all, have been a publicity stunt.

In *Our American Adventure,* Conan Doyle reports that his Buffalo speech was well received, quoting headlines, such as, "Large Audience Profoundly Impressed" and "Sir Arthur Deeply Moves Audience," though it is also not clear where these headlines appeared. Doyle notes that he does not remember "having a better audience than in Buffalo, so alert and sympathetic. It should be so since it was the nearest point to Hydesville at which I spoke," he writes. The real success of the evening, he goes on to note, is that spiritualism is making an effect: "this message of truth and of happiness which alters life and does away with death is finding its way to the people."

From *Our American Adventure,* Chapter IX (1922)

Niagara Electric Power—Under the Falls—Toronto—Remarkable Circle—Sir Donald Mann—The Twentieth Plane—A Liberal Dean—Detroit—American Hotels.

We were greatly interested at Niagara by the new electric-power developments upon the Canadian side. It represents far the greatest thing in this line that has ever been done, and is an example of practical Socialism, as it is financed by a number of municipalities with public money.

As it is costing a good deal more than the estimate, the ratepayers are looking blue, but I expect they will resume their normal colour when the results begin to show, for they expect to get 600,000 horse-power and to run huge factories of all sorts. It should be a national asset.

The idea was to tap the river above the falls, to make a canal 13 miles long, and then to throw this canal down a tube

300 feet deep, until the 20-foot rush of water hits the turbine at the bottom and so converts itself into electric force. They have had smaller plants running both on the American and on the Canadian sides, so there is no question as to the feasibility.

Our whole party put on waterproofs and made its way down the dark and slippery duck-boarded passage which suddenly emerges right under the fall, which roars and spouts in front and on either side of you. Niagara, its colossal strength and impression of might, never has been described and never will be.

Down at the base as much water seems to be ascending from the shock as descending from above, and wild, mad turmoil is the result, which is intensified by the terrible din. To look upwards from the platform and see the sun shine dimly through the great arch of yellow water above you, as through alabaster, is one of the most wonderful impressions in the world.

. . .

It is curious that Niagara, which is probably the chief tourist resort in the world, is singularly weak in hotels. If it were in Switzerland there would be a dozen. As it is, there are only one or two on either bank which can be called decent. The result is that visitors are birds of passage, with no temptation to stay, as they might well do, in that wonderful atmosphere.

They have stretched a wire rope, or several, over the broad expanse of the Whirlpool, and they run a small car across it with passengers. It was an alarming sight for us to see our whole family in this small box suspended hundreds of feet above that dreadful place. However, they made the double transit in all comfort.

Jack London: Not So Civilized

(1876–1916)

Jack London visited Niagara Falls the same year as Arthur Conan Doyle's first visit, in 1894. But while Conan Doyle was already a celebrity, London was unknown, except by the law.

The *Niagara Falls News*, self-described in 1907 as the "official paper of the city," issued a special souvenir publication that year called the *Illustrated Niagara Falls and Its Industries*. The edition's opening article, "An Epitome of American Achievement," describes the city thus:

> Niagara Falls, the beautiful, the sublime, the wonderful, is world-renowned, with its great cataract and development of electrical power, standing as it does, today, in the seventh year of the twentieth century, the grandest and greatest of civilization.[8]

Among its "civilized" infrastructure are libraries, schools, universities, churches, an opera house, railroad lines, a sewage system, electricity, banks, telephone system, newspapers, and a fire department. Absent from this "ideal city in which to locate," is mention of the existence of a police station and courthouse. Jack London would likely beg to differ.

1907 was also the year London published *The Road*, a travel narrative that included his now-infamous visit to Niagara Falls on June 28, 1894, a visit that would last only a night but the consequences of which he paid for over the next month—in the Erie County Penitentiary outside Buffalo, New York.[9] At eighteen, London was not yet famous for adventure stories such as *The Call of the Wild* (1903). He was young, homeless, and facing an unjust system. The lessons he may have learned about being represented as "uncivilized" under the law had not stuck, however, and London's work today is fairly criticized for his own unjust portrayals in some of his fiction.

But in *The Road*, London gives voice to those excluded from mainstream society. His travel narrative details his youthful experiences as a "tramp," a traveling worker and homeless figure who emerged in late-nineteenth-century American society as a product of economic recessions. London's own tramp existence may have been an effect of the financial crisis that began with the Panic of 1893, in which major American companies collapsed, including steel companies, manufacturing industries, and banks. To try to survive, tramps traveled the country's vast railroad network in search of paying jobs. The tramp was a figure often accused of "vagrancy," however—viewed as a criminal due to homelessness rather than any crime committed.[10] London faced such a charge in Niagara Falls, New York, in 1894.

After seeing the Falls, and knowing that vagrancy laws existed, London took the precaution to spend the night outside the city limits. At first light, he ventured again to see the Falls and had just entered the city when he was apprehended. He was charged with vagrancy and within seconds sentenced to thirty days in prison. Neither the apprehending officer nor the court judge would hear his claims of innocence. Like others in his position, his voice would not be heard. In his reflections on his experiences in Niagara Falls, London calls into question the meaning of liberty and justice and what it means to be 'civilized.'

From *The Road* (New York: Macmillan, 1907)

Pinched

I rode into Niagara Falls in a "side-door Pullman," or, in common parlance, a box-car. A flat-car, by the way, is known amongst the fraternity as a "gondola," with the second syllable emphasized and pronounced long. But to return. I arrived in the afternoon and headed straight from the freight train to the falls. Once my eyes were filled with that wonder-vision of down-rushing water, I was lost. (See figure 19.) I could not tear myself away long enough to "batter" the "privates" (domiciles) for my supper. Even a "set-down" could not have lured me away. Night came on, a beautiful night of moonlight, and I lingered by the falls until after eleven. Then it was up to me to hunt for a place to "kip."

"Kip," "doss," "flop," "pound your ear," all mean the same thing; namely, to sleep. Somehow, I had a "hunch" that Niagara Falls was a "bad" town for hoboes, and I headed out into the country. I climbed a fence and "flopped" in a field. John Law would never find me there, I flattered myself. I lay on my back in the grass and slept like a babe.

It was so balmy warm that I woke up not once all night. But with the first gray daylight my eyes opened, and I remembered the wonderful falls. I climbed the fence and started down the road to have another look at them. (See figure 20.) It was early—not more than five o'clock—and not until eight o'clock could I begin to batter for my breakfast. I could spend at least three hours by the river. Alas! I was fated never to see the river nor the falls again.

The town was asleep when I entered it. As I came along the quiet street, I saw three men coming toward me along the

Even a " set-down " could not have lured me away.

Figure 19. Original photograph published in London's *The Road*. New York, Macmillan, 1907. https://catalog.hathitrust.org/Record/000628720.

sidewalk. They were walking abreast. Hoboes, I decided, like myself, who had got up early. In this surmise I was not quite correct. I was only sixty-six and two-thirds per cent correct. The men on each side were hoboes all right, but the man in the middle wasn't. I directed my steps to the edge of the sidewalk in order to let the trio go by. But it didn't go by. At some word from the man in the centre, all three halted, and he of the centre addressed me.

I piped the lay on the instant. He was a "fly-cop" and the two hoboes were his prisoners. John Law was up and out after the early worm. I was a worm. Had I been richer by the experiences that were to befall me in the next several months, I should have turned and run like the very devil. He might have shot at me, but he'd have had to hit me to get me. He'd have never run after me, for two hoboes in the hand are worth more than one on the get-away. But like a dummy I stood still when he halted me. Our conversation was brief.

"What hotel are you stopping at?" he queried.

He had me. I wasn't stopping at any hotel, and, since I did not know the name of a hotel in the place, I could not

Case Closed? / 135

claim residence in any of them. Also, I was up too early in the morning. Everything was against me.

"I just arrived," I said.

"Well, you turn around and walk in front of me, and not too far in front. There's somebody wants to see you."

I was "pinched." I knew who wanted to see me. With that "fly-cop" and the two hoboes at my heels, and under the direction of the former, I led the way to the city jail. There we were searched and our names registered. I have forgotten, now, under which name I was registered. I gave the name of Jack Drake, but when they searched me, they found letters addressed to Jack London. This caused trouble and required explanation, all of which has passed from my mind, and to this day I do not know whether I was pinched as Jack Drake or Jack London. But one or the other, it should be there to-day in the prison register of Niagara Falls. Reference can bring it to light. The time was somewhere in the latter part of June, 1894. It was only a few days after my arrest that the great railroad strike began.

I started down the road.

Figure 20. Original photograph published in London's *The Road*. New York, Macmillan, 1907. https://catalog.hathitrust.org/Record/000628720.

From the office we were led to the "Hobo" and locked in. The "Hobo" is that part of a prison where the minor offenders are confined together in a large iron cage. Since hoboes constitute the principal division of the minor offenders, the aforesaid iron cage is called the Hobo. Here we met several hoboes who had already been pinched that morning, and every little while the door was unlocked and two or three more were thrust in on us. At last, when we totalled sixteen, we were led upstairs into the court-room. And now I shall faithfully describe what took place in that court-room, for now that my patriotic American citizenship there received a shock from which it has never fully recovered.

In the court-room were the sixteen prisoners, the judge, and two bailiffs. The judge seemed to act as his own clerk. There were no witnesses. There were no citizens of Niagara Falls present to look on and see how justice was administered in their community. The judge glanced at the list of cases before him and called out a name. A hobo stood up. The judge glanced at a bailiff. "Vagrancy, your Honor," said the bailiff.

"Thirty days," said his Honor. The hobo sat down, and the judge was calling another name and another hobo was rising to his feet.

The trial of that hobo had taken just about fifteen seconds. The trial of the next hobo came off with equal celerity. The bailiff said, "Vagrancy, your Honor," and his Honor said, "Thirty days." Thus it went like clockwork, fifteen seconds to a hobo—and thirty days.

. . .

And so it went, fifteen seconds and thirty days to each hobo. The machine of justice was grinding smoothly. Most likely, considering how early it was in the morning, his Honor had not yet had his breakfast and was in a hurry.

But my American blood was up. Behind me were the many generations of my American ancestry. One of the kinds of liberty those ancestors of mine had fought and died for was the right of trial by jury. This was my heritage, stained sacred by their blood, and it devolved upon me to stand up for it. All right, I threatened to myself; just wait till he gets to me.

He got to me. My name, whatever it was, was called, and I stood up. The bailiff said, "Vagrancy, your Honor," and I began to talk. But the judge began talking at the same time, and he said, "Thirty days." I started to protest, but at that moment his Honor was calling the name of the next hobo on the list. His Honor paused long enough to say to me, "Shut up!" The bailiff forced me to sit down. And the next moment that next hobo had received thirty days and the succeeding hobo was just in process of getting his.

When we had all been disposed of, thirty days to each stiff, his Honor, just as he was about to dismiss us, suddenly turned to the teamster from Lockport—the one man he had allowed to talk.

"Why did you quit your job?" his Honor asked.

Now the teamster had already explained how his job had quit him, and the question took him aback.

"Your Honor," he began confusedly, "isn't that a funny question to ask?"

"Thirty days more for quitting your job," said his Honor, and the court was closed. That was the outcome. The teamster got sixty days all together, while the rest of us got thirty days.

We were taken down below, locked up, and given breakfast. It was a pretty good breakfast, as prison breakfasts go, and it was the best I was to get for a month to come. . . .

We were all handcuffed similarly, in pairs. This accomplished, a bright nickel-steel chain was brought forth, run down through the links of all the handcuffs, and locked at front and rear of the double-line. We were now a chain-gang. The command to march was given, and out we went upon the street, guarded by two officers. The tall negro and I had the place of honor. We led the procession.

After the tomb-like gloom of the jail, the outside sunshine was dazzling. I had never known it to be so sweet as now, a prisoner with clanking chains, I knew that I was soon to see the last of it for thirty days. Down through the streets of Niagara Falls we marched to the railroad station, stared at by curious passers-by, and especially by a group of tourists on the veranda of a hotel that we marched past. . . .

The train stopped at a station about five miles from Buffalo, and we, the chain-gang, got off. . . .

We left the car, walked some more, and were led into the office of the Erie County Penitentiary. Here we were to register, and on that register one or the other of my names will be found.

. . .

Early next morning our cells were unlocked, and down in the hall the several hundred prisoners of us formed the lock-step and marched out into the prison-yard to go to work. The Erie Canal runs right by the back yard of the Erie County Penitentiary. Our task was to unload canal-boats, carrying huge stay-bolts on our shoulders, like railroad ties, into the prison. As I worked I sized up the situation and studied the chances for a get-away. There wasn't the ghost of a show. Along the tops of the walls marched guards armed with repeating rifles, and I was told, furthermore, that there were machine-guns in the sentry-towers. . . .

What had I done? What crime had I committed against the good citizens of Niagara Falls that all this vengeance should be wreaked upon me? I had not even violated their "sleeping-out" ordinance. I had slept outside their jurisdiction, in the country, that night. I had not even begged for a meal, or battered for a "light piece" on their streets. All that I had done was to walk along their sidewalk and gaze at their picayune waterfall. And what crime was there in that? Technically I was guilty of no misdemeanor. All right, I'd show them when I got out. . . .

As the days went by, however, I began to grow convinced. I saw with my own eyes, there in that prison, things unbelievable and monstrous. And the more convinced I became, the profounder grew the respect in me for the sleuth-hounds of the law and for the whole institution of criminal justice.

My indignation ebbed away, and into my being rushed the tides of fear. I saw at last, clear-eyed, what I was up against. I grew meek and lowly. Each day I resolved more emphatically to make no rumpus when I got out. All I asked, when I got out, was a chance to fade away from the landscape. And that was just what I did do when I was released. I kept my tongue between my teeth, walked softly, and sneaked for Pennsylvania, a wiser and a humbler man.

Chapter 10

Save Niagara

*S*ince at least Fr. Hennepin, explorers, empires, entrepreneurs, and engineers have interpreted the magnificence of the Falls, with their mist rising over the canopy, as a beacon of conquest. Native American portage routes, used for transport, trade, and livelihood, were early claimed and widened to accommodate white settlement of the region, and by the first quarter of the eighteenth century, a mill was built on Niagara's brink. Over the next century, hotels and tourist attractions, industry and canals further carved the landscape, soon followed by steamboats and steam engines, railroads and suspension bridges, all in the name of "progress." The contrast between nature and technology was not only visible by the nineteenth century, but arguments over which was the more "sublime" had begun. At stake was the future of the Falls.

With the dominance of industrial mills and tourist attractions at the Falls by the 1870s, environmental advocates agitated to preserve its natural beauty and restorative power in what came to be known as the "Free Niagara Movement." The preservationists triumphed, and by the mid-1880s, green public spaces were established on both sides of the border—the Niagara Reservation Park, now the Niagara Falls State Park on the American side, and the Queen Victoria Park on the Canadian side. But while much of Niagara's scenery was preserved for the tourist, the greater surrounding region, including the water itself, was claimed by industrialists looking to improve the efficiency of their mills and plants by utilizing the power of the Falls.[1]

While hydraulic power from diverted water was used as early as 1861, it would not generate electricity for another two decades, at the time the Free Niagara Movement was beginning to reshape the landscape. In another decade and a half, in 1896, the longest transmission of electric power reached Buffalo, New York from Niagara Falls. The generation of electricity prompted another battle between nature preservationists and proponents of water diversion for power. When H. G. Wells arrived in 1906, the "Save Niagara" protest to limit the quantity of diverted water from the Falls was at its height.

H. G. Wells: War of the Words

(1866–1946)

For a writer of science fiction in books such as The Time Machine *(1895) and* The War of the Worlds *(1898), it is little wonder that H. G. Wells traveled to America at the start of the twentieth century to write a book he had already titled* The Future in America: A Search after Realities *(1906). In it, he would enter the great debate of whether to "Save Niagara" for nature or for technology.*

Prior to his American tour in the spring of 1906, Herbert George Wells wrote to his friend, the novelist Henry James, for letters of introduction to take with him to America. Wells was going, he tells James in a January letter, "to write loose large articles mingled with impressions of *The Future in America* (no less)."[2] What Wells meant by the "no less" crouched between parentheses can only be speculated. Is it a commitment made to himself about what he hoped to achieve? Is it a sign of self-doubt, however subtle? Is it a way of letting James know, sheepishly, that Wells, too, was writing a travel book on America? After all, James himself was busy compiling a collection of travel essays titled *The American Scene*.

James read Wells's book when it appeared in November that year. Writer, critic, and friend, James compares their work. Where James complicates, Wells enviously simplifies. Where James's book is not published until the start of 1907, Wells works quickly. Where James is a creature of the past, Wells focuses on the future. Where James is quiet, Wells shouts. And it's shouting that's needed, James acknowledges. Oscar Wilde said that "America is the noisiest country that ever existed."[3] As James puts it to Wells, America is "a yelling country, and the voice must pierce or dominate; and *my* semitones, in your splendid clashing of the cymbals (and *theirs*,) will never be heard."[4]

Henry James had long before expressed his view of Niagara Falls. For James, the Falls were all that landscape tourists and artists had sought: the picturesque and the beautiful. The Falls were "order, proportion and symmetry." But even more, they were a place where the natural world gave way to the divine, a place of spiritual transcendence. Where James and Wells did agree was on the ruin of the Falls by the many buildings, signs, and tourist attractions. As Wells declares: "For the most part these accumulations of human effort about Niagara are extremely defiling and ugly . . . offensive to the eye." But, he argues, these eyesores only represent a state in flux. In the progress toward hydroelectric power, with is its vast "dynamos and turbines," the real beauty and transcendence at the Falls lay in technology. To focus on the picturesque or natural beauty, according to Wells, is to miss out on what other creative uses the Falls can inspire.

Wells arrived at the Falls at a moment when newspaper articles and editorials were inflamed with the topic of how to "save Niagara"—to develop its hydroelectric power by diverting water and changing its landscape. His essay on Niagara first appeared on Saturday, July 21, 1906, in an issue of *Harper's Weekly*. Wells's view was loud and clear: hydroelectric power surpasses the natural sublimity of the Falls. But not all agreed.

In a war of words, an editorial in *Goodwin's Weekly* critiqued Wells's "quantitative" assessment of the Falls. The writer of "Save Niagara" demonstrates the anger this debate aroused. Referring to Wells (albeit unnamed in the editorial), the writer comments: "The man's bump of sublimity or his imagination is dimmed," since he "really seems more impressed with man's work there than with God's." After blasting Wells with this harsh criticism, the editorialist nevertheless goes on to admit that perhaps Wells is right—perhaps the machinery of Niagara is more sublime than its natural elements. Readers might buy into the idea of lessening "the glory of Niagara" by diverting its water for utilitarian purpose. "But no, no," the writer concludes: "It will be a sin for the cupidity of man to mar that work of the Infinite." To advocate for technological uses of the Falls is a prideful "sin," the letter writer contends.

But to many tourists, the "glory" of Niagara was as much a product of the technological sublime as the natural. Tourism had not lessened. The caption to the image attending Wells's essay on Niagara in *Harper's Weekly* echoes the writer's focus on "quantity" in his assessment of the power of water and electricity generation at the Falls. (See figure 21.) What both the author and illustrator seem to have missed, however, is that the tourists depicted are stepping out into nature, not into the tunnels and dynamos that so impressed Wells.

>From *The Future in America:*
A Search after Realities (1906)

"The End of Niagara"

Everywhere in the America I have seen the same note sound, the note of a fatal gigantic economic development, of large prevision and enormous pressures.

I heard it clear above the roar of Niagara—for, after all, I stopped off at Niagara.

As a water-fall, Niagara's claim to distinction is now mainly quantitative; its spectacular effect, its magnificent and humbling size and splendor, were long since destroyed beyond recovery by the hotels, the factories, the power-houses, the bridges and tramways and hoardings that arose about it. It must have been a fine thing to happen upon suddenly after a day of solitary travel; the Indians, they say, gave it worship; but it's no great wonder to reach it by trolley-car, through a street hack-infested and full of adventurous refreshment-places and souvenir-shops and the touting guides. There were great quantities of young couples and other sightseers with the usual encumbrances of wrap and bag and umbrella, trailing out across the bridges and along the neat paths of the Reservation Parks, asking the way to this point and that. Notice boards cut the eye, offering extra joys and memorable objects for twenty-five and fifty cents, and it was proposed you should keep off the grass.

. . .

No doubt the Falls, seen from the Canadian side, have a peculiar long majesty of effect; but the finest thing in it all, to my mind, was not Niagara at all, but to look up-stream from Goat Island and see the sea-wide crest of the flashing sunlit rapids against the gray-blue sky. That was like a limitless ocean pouring down a sloping world towards one, and I lingered, held by that, returning to it through an indolent afternoon. It gripped

Figure 21. H. G. Wells's "The End of Niagara," illustration in *The Future in America: A Search after Realities*, Saturday, July 21, 1906, issue of *Harper's Weekly* L, no. 2587.

the imagination as nothing else there seemed to do. It was so broad an infinitude of splash and hurry. And, moreover, all the enterprising hotels and expectant trippers were out of sight.

That was the best of the display. The real interest of Niagara for me, was not in the water-fall but in the human accumulations about it. They stood for the future, threats and promises, and the water-fall was just a vast reiteration of falling water. The note of growth in human accomplishment rose clear and triumphant above the elemental thunder.

For the most part these accumulations of human effort about Niagara are extremely defiling and ugly. Nothing—not even the hotel signs and advertisement boards—could be more offensive to the eye and mind than the Schoellkopf Company's untidy confusion of sheds and buildings on the American side, wastefully squirting out long, tail-race cascades below the bridge, and nothing more disgusting than the sewer-pipes and gas-work ooze that the town of Niagara Falls contributes to the scenery. But, after all, these represent only the first slovenly onslaught of mankind's expansion, the pioneers' camp of the human-growth process that already changes its quality and manner. There are finer things than these outrages to be found.

The dynamos and turbines of the Niagara Falls Power Company, for example, impressed me far more profoundly than the Cave of the Winds; are, indeed, to my mind, greater and more beautiful than that accidental eddying of air beside a downpour. They are will made visible, thought translated into easy and commanding things. They are clean, noiseless, and starkly powerful. All the clatter and tumult of the early age of machinery is past and gone here; there is no smoke, no coal grit, no dirt at all. The wheel-pit into which one descends has an almost cloistered quiet about its softly humming turbines. These are altogether noble masses of machinery, huge black slumbering monsters, great sleeping tops that engender irresistible forces in their sleep. They sprang, armed like Minerva, from serene and speculative, foreseeing and endeavoring brains. First was the word and then these powers. A man goes to and fro quietly in the long, clean hall of the dynamos. There is no clangor, no racket. Yet the outer rim of the big generators is spinning at the pace of a hundred thousand miles an hour; the dazzling clean switch-board, with its little handles and levers, is the seat of empire over more power than the strength of a million disciplined, unquestioning men. All these great things are as silent, as wonderfully made, as the heart in a living body, and stouter and stronger than that. . . .

When I thought that these two huge wheel-pits of this company are themselves but a little intimation of what can be done in this way, what will be done in this way, my imagination towered above me. I fell into a day-dream of the coming power of men, and how that power may be used by them. . . .

For surely the greatness of life is still to come, it is not in such accidents as mountains or the sea. I have seen the splendor of the mountains, sunrise and sunset among them, and the waste immensity of sky and sea. I am not blind because I can see beyond these glories. To me no other thing is credible than that all the natural beauty in the world is only so much material for the imagination and the mind, so many hints and suggestions for art and creation. Whatever is, is but the lure and symbol towards what can be willed and done. Man lives to make—in the end he must make, for there will be nothing else left for him to do.

And the world he will make—after a thousand years or so!

I, at least, can forgive the loss of all the accidental, unmeaning beauty that is going for the sake of the beauty of fine order and intention that will come. I believe—passionately, as a doubting lover believes in his mistress—in the future of mankind. And so to me it seems altogether well that all the froth and hurry of Niagara at last, all of it, dying into hungry canals of intake, should rise again in light and power, in ordered and equipped and proud and beautiful humanity, in cities and palaces and the emancipated souls and hearts of men. . . .

There is much discussion about Niagara at present. It may be some queer compromise, based on the pretense that a voluminous water-fall is necessarily a thing of incredible beauty, and a human use is necessarily a degrading use, will "save" Niagara and the hack-drivers and the souvenir-shops for series of years yet, "a magnificent monument to the pride of the United States in a glory of nature," as one journalistic savior puts it. It is, as public opinion stands, a quite conceivable thing. This electric development may be stopped after all, and the huge fall of water remain surrounded by gravel paths and parapets and geranium-beds, a staring-point for dull wonder, a crown for a day's excursion, a thunderous impressive accessory to the vulgar love-making that fills the surrounding hotels, a Titanic imbecility of wasted gifts. But I don't think so. I think somebody will pay something, and the journalistic zeal for scenery abate. I think the huge social and industrial process of America will win in this conflict, and at last capture Niagara altogether.

And then—what use will it make of its prey?

Epilogue

Still Seeing Niagara

*I*n 1979, geographer Peirce Lewis wrote that landscapes are "our unwitting autobiography." Perhaps because "place" is a human construct—barren space until we stamp it with our mark, our memories, our meaning—place is also contested space, as geographer and poet Tim Cresswell more recently suggests.[1] Arthur Lumley represented this concept in 1873 in the illustration that opens this book, *Niagara Seen with Different Eyes*, with its conflicting views of the landscape.

Though arguably still iconic, Niagara Falls may no longer be *the* symbol, as it once was, of the New World, of the sublime, of natural and unnatural power. In many ways it symbolizes all that has been lost or taken—from indigenous lands to natural vistas we can never recapture. Though its resources have not been depleted, its aura may be, in the overexposure of mechanical and digital reproduction, selfie and Instagrammable culture, and in the environmental mishaps of aging water disposal and other facilities in recent years.

Despite all of this, millions still are drawn to the Falls each year. Throughout the twentieth and now into the twenty-first centuries, writers have continued to express what at times seems inexpressible and to capture untold stories of the Falls. The prevailing genres of the nineteenth century, the intensity of the poetic image and the personal experience of travel narratives, have given way to novels and short stories in recent decades. In work by canonical, mainstream, regional and indigenous authors, the Falls persist as a character, symbol, and setting in literature of the present, reinscribing the landscape we thought we knew and waiting for a reader.

Notes

Acknowledgments

1. Lumley may be best known for his Civil War illustrations.

Introduction

1. Ralph Waldo Emerson, letter dated January 8, 1863. *The Letters of Ralph Waldo Emerson*, vol. 5, *1856–1867*, ed. Ralph L. Rusk (New York: Columbia University Press, 1939), 304.

2. Emerson had met Lincoln a year earlier through Secretary of State, William H. Seward of Auburn, New York, and had for nearly two decades held abolitionist views. Seward would later help Harriet Tubman to establish a home in Auburn, New York.

3. Emerson, letter dated January 8, 1863. *The Letters of Ralph Waldo Emerson*, vol. 5: *1856–1867*, 304.

4. *Niagara Gazette*, Wednesday, January 7, 1863, no. 454, roll #12, *NF Gazette*-Weekly, January 7, 1863–December 30, 1863. Niagara Falls Public Library.

5. The first Suspension Bridge was built in 1848 for pedestrians and carriages. By 1855, the bridge began to accommodate railroad thanks to the design of John A. Roebling, who two decades later would design the iconic Brooklyn Bridge.

6. The superintendent was Reuben Rice. The quotation is taken from Ralph Rusk's *The Life of Ralph Waldo Emerson* (New York: Scribner's Sons, 1949), 418–19. On his lecture tours, Emerson kept logs of his traveling expenses, recorded in a small journal. The ticket he lost in the fire for the trip from Buffalo to Chicago would have cost no small amount. Emerson's journal from 1850 provides a record of his potential losses, which include rates from Albany to Buffalo and Niagara Falls. The record also provides insight into how Emerson spent a brief excursion at the Falls.

Tickets to Buffalo		9.75
Expenses		75
Phelps's Buffalo		1.00
Ticket to & from Falls		1.00
Ticket at Falls	25	
d[itt]o	25	
suspension	25	
Cab	25	
ferry	6	
dinner	<u>50</u>	1.56
Niagara book		.25

See Ralph Waldo Emerson, *The Journals and Miscellaneous Notebooks of Ralph Waldo Emerson*, vol. 11: *1848–1851*, ed. A. W. Plumstead, William H. Gilman, and Ruth H. Bennett (Cambridge, MA: The Belknap Press of Harvard University Press, 1975), 535.

    7. Coincidentally, just over a decade earlier, Emerson was on board a steamboat from Buffalo to Cleveland, similarly named *America*, and which also caught fire. Emerson is more composed when he writes of this earlier brush with death in a letter to his brother William, written from Cincinnati on May 29, 1850: "I have been here more than a week, having escaped burning in the 'America,' which was pretty well on fire when we touched Cleveland." The steamer had caught fire in the boiler room. According to the *Cleveland Daily Plain Dealer*, "The Captain very discreetly told the firemen to keep their places, not to alarm the passengers, and prepare themselves with buckets." This discretion may account for Emerson's unflappable response. Despite his calm, however, the story could have turned out much worse, as the newspaper article explains: She [the *America*] was considerably charred and no doubt would have burned up had she been at sea or in any place where an efficient fire department could not have assisted her."

    Fortunately, both the vessel and Emerson survived with "little damage." Indeed, Emerson was unscathed by the event and closes his letter to William with a note of optimism for having "seen Niagara [& so] the time is not wholly lost." Ralph Waldo Emerson, *The Letters of Ralph Waldo Emerson*, vol. 4: *1848–1855*, ed. Ralph L. Rusk (New York: Columbia University Press, 1939), 270. "The American on Fire," *Cleveland Daily Plain Dealer*, May 16, 1850.

    8. *Niagara Gazette*, Wednesday, January 7, 1863, no. 454, roll #12, *NF Gazette*-Weekly January 7, 1863–December 30, 1863. Niagara Falls Public Library.

    9. By the mid-nineteenth century, as Karen Dubinksy puts it, "in this first period of prestigious tourism, celebrity tourists helped make Niagara a cultural icon" (37). *The Second Greatest Disappointment: Honeymooning and Tourism at Niagara Falls* (New Brunswick, NJ: Rutgers University Press, 1999).

10. Charles Mason Dow. *Anthology and Bibliography of Niagara Falls,* vols. 1 and 2 (Albany, NY: J. B. Lyon Co., 1921). Local History Department, Niagara Falls Public Library. 1–2.

11. In *A Skeptic's Guide to Writers' Houses*, Anne Trubek points out that because "writers produce art that is easily reproducible and accessible, but offer no common meeting spot, gathering place or shrine-ready structure," writer's homes and graves, if deemed worthy of preservation, become de facto sites of literary worship, places where readers try to render present their reading experiences. Anne Trubek, *A Skeptic's Guide to Writers' Houses* (Philadelphia: University of Pennsylvania Press, 2011), 5.

12. One can visit, for example, in St. Catharines, Ontario, the Salem Chapel, British Methodist Episcopal Church, where Harriet Tubman was a member in the 1850s. Further afield is the Rev. Josiah Henson's Homestead in Dresden, Ontario. In Guelph, Ontario, is World War I soldier poet John McCrae's house; and in Buffalo, New York, the Buffalo and Erie County Public Library hosts the Mark Twain Room, including items from Twain's Buffalo home from 1870 to 1871, and the manuscript of *Adventures of Huckleberry Finn*. In our own present, we might seek out where Joyce Carol Oates grew up in Lockport, New York.

13. The Porter family first built a wooden walkway in 1827, on the American edge of Horseshoe Falls off Goat Island across the large stones jutting out of the water like the shells of terrapin turtles. In 1833 they added the tower, over thirty feet in height, with a winding staircase leading up to a lookout.

14. The stairs descending into the gorge were largely financed in 1829 by Nicholas Biddle, lawyer and president of the nation's second central bank.

15. The earliest *written* mention of the Falls appears in the early seventeenth century, as reported by Indians to European explorers. The first European to see the Falls firsthand and to write an account of that experience does not appear until the final quarter of that century.

16. Because this book is part anthology, the texts included were published before 1923 and so are in the public domain. While I would very much like to have included contemporary works on the Falls throughout the twentieth century and into the present, the project would become too different to the present version and too prohibitive in terms of copyright. In addition, it was beyond the scope of this current book to include international writers beyond the British and Irish authors included here.

17. It is not certain when Porter's poem was originally written, though the lines that would become the poem's refrain were written while he was an undergraduate at Harvard University in the early 1840s. Though this poem appears in *Niagara: Its 1872 History and Geology, Incidents and Poetry*, other poems of Porter's were published in periodicals. Michelle Kratts at the Lewiston, New York Public Library has located several of these poems and assembled copies for

the library's Local History collection. On Porter's life at Harvard, see my article, "Col. Peter A. Porter and the Emersons" in *WNY Heritage Magazine* 21, no. 1 (Spring 2018): 8–21.

Chapter 1

1. Hennepin was an adventurer who was sent in 1675 to "New France" to assess French colonies along the St. Lawrence River, present-day Quebec, with the famous explorer René-Robert Cavelier de La Salle. Hennepin was then sent to present-day Kingston, Ontario, as a missionary, and in 1678 to the Niagara region before departing to explore the Mississippi River region. His first book *Description de la Louisiane*, published in 1683, included his first mention of the Falls of Niagara.

2. The full title of Hennepin's book was *A New Discovery of a Vast Country in America, Extending above Four Thousand Miles, between New France and New Mexico. With a Description of the Great Lakes, Cataracts, Rivers, Plants, and Animals: Also, the Manners, Customs, and Languages, of the Several Native Indians; and the Advantage of Commerce with Those Different Nations.* "Discovery" was the means by which lands were colonized, peoples enslaved and indigenous nations removed.

3. Leo Marx discusses these conflicting images in *The Machine in the Garden* (1964) (New York: Oxford University Press, 2000).

4. Laura Donaldson quoted in Phillip H. Round, *Removable Type: Histories of the Book in Indian Country, 1663–1880* (Chapel Hill: University of North Carolina Press, 2010), 11.

5. See Richard Gassan, *The Birth of American Tourism: New York, the Hudson Valley, and American Culture, 1790-1835* (Amherst: University of Massachusetts Press, 2008).

6. The Northern or "Fashionable Tour" was imitative of the "Grand Tour" of the Old World, which took the English aristocracy and gentry to sites of classical culture and centers of art, such as France, Italy, and Greece.

7. Sedgwick would be included, with Washington Irving, James Fenimore Cooper, Ralph Waldo Emerson, and Nathaniel Hawthorne, in the first book devoted to literary tourism in the US: *Homes of American Authors, Comprising Anecdotical, Personal, and Descriptive Sketches*, published in 1853.

8. From the late 1770s to the early 1830s, European settlers called the area around the Falls "Stamford," then later, the villages of Drumondville and Clifton, which were incorporated as the City of Niagara Falls, Ontario, Canada, in 1904.

9. By 1832, the fee was 50 cents. Forsyth's legal troubles can be found in Robert L. Fraser "William Forsyth" in *Provincial Justice: Upper Canadian Legal*

Portraits from the Dictionary of Canadian Biography, edited by Robert L. Fraser (Toronto: University of Toronto Press, 1992), 385.

10. Richard H. Gassan notes that Sedgwick was later "skeptical" of the tourism industry, as evidenced in her 1825 book, *The Travellers: A Tale Designed for Young People*, because it distanced people from more spiritual appreciation of places like Niagara Falls. Gassan *The Birth of American Tourism*, 137. Quotations from Sedgwick's "The Catholic Iroquois" are from *Sedgwick Stories: The Periodical Writings of Catharine Maria Sedgwick*. https://sedgwickstories.omeka.net/items/show/32.

11. Sedgwick, "The Catholic Iroquois."

12. Sedgwick likely stayed in Lewiston, New York on July 2, 1821, before departing from Youngstown by steamboat on July 3. Catharine Maria Sedgwick, *Life and Letters of Catharine M. Sedgwick*, ed. Mary Dewey (New York: Harper, 1871).

13. Already by her first publication in 1822, Sedgwick was critical of missionary work to evangelize members of the Cherokee nation.

14. Maureen Konkle, *Writing Indian Nations: Native Intellectuals and the Politics of Historiography, 1827–1863*, 4. Daniel Radus helpfully notes in "Printing Native History in David Cusick's *Sketches of Ancient History of the Six Nations*": "small-press printing coincided with the height of land speculation and its attendant resistance" (226).

15. Round, *Removable Type*, 150. Native autobiographies, histories, and newspapers followed the 1770 publication. Cusick's title included this notable subheading: —*Comprising—First a Tale of the Foundation of the Great Island, (Now North America)*.

16. Konkle, *Writing Indian Nations*, 15.

17. From the *Daily National Journal* (Washington, DC), Saturday, July 7, 1827; issue 887. Gale Document Number:GT3012498261; syndicated in other regional newspapers.

18. The publication identifies the "Onguys" as the Iroquois, the name used by Europeans for the Six Nations or Haudensaunee. *Atlantic Journal, and Friend of Knowledge* 1, nos. 1–8 (1833): 34.

19. Letter 416 in Margaret Fuller, *The Letters of Margaret Fuller*, vol. 3: *1842–44*, ed. Robert N. Hudspeth (Ithaca, NY: Cornell University Press, 1984), 130–31.

20. In a published edition of excerpts from the albums, G. W. Holley notes of this poem, "Thoughts on Visiting Niagara," that it is "the most popular of the facetious rhymes about Niagara" (156). In *Niagara: Its 1872 History and Geology, Incidents and Poetry*, Holley publishes the first stanza thus:

> I wonder how long you've been a roarin'
> At this infernal rate.
> I wonder if all you've been a pourin'
> Could be ciphered on a slate.

21. In a letter dated "Niagara 30th May [18]43," Fuller describes to her friend, Elizabeth Hoar, the twenty-four-hour trip: "ceaseless, steady motion, the gentle dripping of the rain, snatches of low talk among the passengers, but just seen by the one lamp on some mysterious subject, which speedily mingled with a dream, then occasionally to hear 'We are passing Genesee river' and the like and make pictures of these unseen places. The whole night has to me the effect of phantasmagoria, as I look back" (Letter 413). Fuller was able to recline on the train-car couches, but got little sleep and was grateful when she had time to rest in Buffalo before the journey north to Niagara. Fuller, *The Letters of Margaret Fuller*, vol. 3, 126.

22. See, for example, 57th Annual Report of the Regents of the University, to the Legislature of the State of New York (Albany: University of the State of New York). Board of Regents, 1844: "A NOTED DAY.—June 1, 1843.—The first of June, 1843, will long be remembered. Snow fell in Buffalo and Rochester. In this vicinity ice was formed" (232).

23. Built in 1825 on the brink of the American Falls, the three-story Cataract House was a popular destination for tourists, particularly the wealthy and well known. It was also an important site on the Underground Railroad, which can be experienced at the Niagara Falls Underground Railroad Heritage Center.

24. Fuller begins this letter to Emerson, dated "1 June 1843, Niagara": "I send you a token, made by the hands of some Seneca Indian lady. If you use it for a watch-pocket, hang it, when you travel, at the head of your bed, and you may dream of Niagara. If you use it for a purse, you can put in it alms for poets and artists" (Letter 415). Margaret Fuller, *The Letters of Margaret Fuller*, vol. 3, 128.

Seneca, Tuscarora and Mohawk all sold handmade items at the Falls. A decade before Fuller, Hawthorne similarly made a purchase from local Tuscarora sellers. Tuscarora and other Six Nations women continued to sell beadwork purses, pincushions, picture frames, and other handcrafted items throughout the height of nineteenth century tourism. Tourists consumed the souvenirs as part of their "authentic" experience of the Falls, romanticizing the Native sellers as part of the "natural" landscape. Elsewhere in her text, Fuller problematically associates the sublime feeling of the Falls with a fantasized image of a "noble savage" in the wilderness. For more on Tuscarora beadwork at the Falls, see Gerry Biron, *The Cherished Curiosity: The Souvenir Beaded Bag in Historic Haudenosaunee (Iroquois Art)* (Brainerd, Minnesota: Bang Printing, 2012); and Beverly Gordon, "Souvenirs of Niagara Falls: The Significance of Indian Whimsies," *New York History* 67, no. 4 (October 1986): 389–409.

25. Joan von Mehren notes that major themes in *Summer on the Lakes* include "the dislocation and disjointedness that western settlement had forced on the lives of the newcomers and the Native Americans alike. She mourns the despoiling of the land and the displacement of the Indians, the insensitivity of the newcomers to natural beauty and to human suffering, the futility of the settlers' clinging to old identities and forms in the new environment." See Joan von

Mehren, *Minerva and the Muse: A Life of Margaret Fuller* (Amherst: University of Massachusetts Press, 1994), 179.

26. Now the spa-town called *Bad Muskau*, which is located on the German-Polish border.

27. See Peter James Bowman, *The Fortune Hunter: A German Prince in Regency England*, 35. Later, Pückler's wife opened a spa on the premises, including a chateau and bathhouse, and "landscaping" that would eventually sink the couple into so much debt in the 1820s that the only solution they could foresee was to divorce and for the Prince to go to England in search of a wealthy new wife.

28. When brothers Peter and Augustus Porter petitioned New York State for the purchase of the largest island between the Falls in 1816, the state terminated the Seneca title to Goat Island and sold it to the Porters. The island, it was claimed, was to be used for the purpose of raising sheep, which would be kept safe from wolves and other predators by the barrier of the rapids. The Porters' construction of a wooden bridge in 1817 soon proved more lucrative than the island, however. Visitors had to pay a toll to get to the island for its view of the Falls. By early 1818, heavy ice down the Niagara River dislodged the bridge. Within months, the Porters rebuilt a stronger wooden bridge, which cost $2,000, according to an 1843 guidebook, the year of Fuller's visit. By 1839, the wood had begun to rot, necessitating a third bridge, which now cost $3,000. (This bridge was eventually replaced with iron in 1855.)

29. See Winifred Morgan, *An American Icon: Brother Jonathan and American Identity* (Newark: University of Delaware Press, 1988), 17; 23.

30. Jack Downing, created by humorist Seba Smith in the 1830s, was, like the Jonathan figure, similarly naive, yet usefully shrewd. Though hailing from the rural and fictional "Downingville," Downing ambitiously makes his way to the US capital, eventually becoming enmeshed in politics. Smith uses the character to satirize President Andrew Jackson and his administration.

31. Biographer Megan Marshall reads Fuller's use of the chained eagle to refer symbolically to the forced displacement of the Cherokee Nation. *Margaret Fuller: A New American Life* (Boston, MA: Mariner Books, 2013), 204.

32. Fuller's phrasing here refers to an 1837 poem by James Bird titled "Francis Abbot, the Recluse of Niagara." Abbot lived in an old cabin on Goat Island from 1829 to 1831, when he died going over the Falls.

Chapter 2

1. From Samuel DeVeaux *The Traveller's Own Book, to Saratoga Springs, Niagara Falls and Canada* (Buffalo, NY: Faxon & Co., 1841), 172.

2. Studies in the cognitive sciences, from cognitive psychology to neurobiology, are demonstrating the transformative effects, for instance, of walking in

nature, and its improvement on mental and emotional health, creativity, and compassion. With the help of electroencephalograms (EEGs) and functional Magnetic Resonance Imaging (fMRIs) as well as newer technologies, scientists can study how the brain's neurons and networks respond to environmental stimuli. And this is not just "green" nature, but "blue" as well, as Wallace J. Nichols argues in *Blue Mind: The Surprising Science That Shows How Being Near, In, or Under Water Can Make You Happier, Healthier, More Connected, and Better at What You Do* (2014).

3. From Pierre M. Irving, *The Life and Letters of Washington Irving*, vol. 1 (New York: Putnam, 1864). Reprint (Detroit, MI: Gale Research Co., 1967).

4. See Andrew Burstein, *The Original Knickerbocker: The Life of Washington Irving* (New York: Basic Books, 2007). And *Washington Irving Letters*, vol. 2, *1823–1838*, eds. Ralph M. Aderman, Herbert L. Kleinfield, and Jenifer S. Banks (Boston: Twayne Publishers, 1979), 709.

5. Irving's traveling companions were the British Charles Joseph Latrobe and the Swiss Albert-Alexandre de Pourtalès, whom he had met on his voyage home from Europe.

6. Like Margaret Fuller and Henry David Thoreau after him, Irving's tour of the West included surveying the state of Indian nations who had been displaced through removal policies of the 1830s.

7. Velvet Nelson, *An Introduction to the Geography of Tourism* (Lanham, MD: Rowman and Littlefield Publishers, 2013), 86.

8. See G. F. Pyle, "The Diffusion of Cholera in the United States in the Nineteenth Century," *Geographical Analysis* 1, no. 1 (January 1969): 59–75; and Ashleigh R. Tuite, Christina H. Chan, and David N. Fisman, "Cholera, Canals, and Contagion: Rediscovering Dr. Beck's Report," *Journal of Public Health Policy* 32, no. 3: 320–33.

9. Washington Irving, *Washington Irving Journals and Notebooks*, vol. 5, *1832–1859*, ed. Sue Fields Ross (Boston: Twayne Publishers, 1986), 7.

10. *Washington Irving Letters*, vol. 2, *1823–1838*, eds. Ralph M. Aderman, Herbert L. Kleinfield, and Jenifer S. Banks (Boston: Twayne Publishers, 1979), 711, 716–17.

11. See "The Great Wonder of the Canal" in Janet Dorothy Larkin, *Overcoming Niagara: Canals, Commerce, and Tourism in the Niagara-Great Lakes Borderland Region, 1792–1837* (Albany: State University of New York Press, 2018), 143–75. Larkin notes, for instance, that "For those crossing the Ridge Road in route to Niagara during the Erie Canal's building, they would have been fascinated by the supplies of gunpowder, animals, workers and other provisions being transported along the road to Lockport where excavation was going forward on the much publicized Lockport Locks, an engineering marvel that became another anticipated attraction on the Erie Canal" (155).

12. Irving notes that they "take an extra there & continue on to Niagara" (21). Irving, *Washington Irving Journals and Notebooks*, vol. 5, *1832–1859*.

13. The Irving citations are from Pierre M. Irving, *The Life and Letters of Washington Irving*, vol. 1 (New York: Putnam, 1864). Reprint (Detroit, MI: Gale Research Co., 1967), 157–59.

14. Killis Campbell, "The Kennedy Papers: A Sheaf of Unpublished Letters from Washington Irving," *Sewanee Review* 25, no. 1 (January, 1917): 1–19. Accessed May 31, 2018.

15. Irving's drawing, figure 5, with its rough outlines of the Falls, captures this sense of immediacy—what Leo Marx calls "joyous fulfillment" in the "new land" (42–43). Leo Marx, *The Machine in the Garden* (1964) (New York: Oxford University Press, 2000). According to Sue Fields Ross, Irving annotated the drawing thus: "1 Sea green & transparent"; "2 intensely white & brilliant"; "in the center of the page are the words, 'light gauzy mist'" (31–32). *Washington Irving: Journals and Notebooks*, vol. 5, 1832–1859, ed. Sue Fields Ross (Twayne Author's Series, 1986).

16. Washington Irving, *Washington Irving Journals and Notebooks*, vol. 5, *1832–1859*.

17. Marx, *The Machine in the Garden*, 197.

18. Henry David Thoreau, *The Journal: 1837–1861*, ed. Damion Searls (New York: New York Review Books, 2009), 23.

19. See, for example, Ray Angelo, "Thoreau as Botanist: An Appreciation and a Critique." *The Thoreau Quarterly* (1984) 15. 13–23.

20. Thoreau had possibly caught his cold from Bronson Alcott. The two had met to plan a memorial for the abolitionist John Brown, on the first anniversary of his execution, as they had done a year earlier, a continuance of protest that had nevertheless failed to get Brown clemency from the US government. Thoreau knew and was close friends with some of the "Secret Six" who had funded Brown's raid on Harpers Ferry, an attempt to incite a slave rebellion. In the weeks after Brown's imprisonment, Thoreau wrote "Plea for Captain John Brown," the first public defense of Brown's actions. On November 1, 1860, Thoreau was asked to deliver this speech in Boston. He was a replacement for Frederick Douglass, who was on his way to Canada, and may have been in Niagara Falls at the time. Douglass had been inadvertently implicated in Harpers Ferry when a letter from Douglass was found in Brown's pocket. Douglass, however, had opposed Brown's plans. See Laura Dassow Walls, *Henry David Thoreau: A Life* (Chicago: University of Chicago Press, 2017), 475. Also Corinne Hosfeld Smith, *Westward I Go Free: Tracing Thoreau's Last Journey* (Winnipeg, MB: Green Frigate Books, 2012); and Bill Bradberry, "Black Menagerie: Home Again—Taking the Scenic Route," *Niagara Falls Reporter*, July 23, 2002. http://niagarafallsreporter.com/menagerie59.html.

21. Leo Marx helpfully notes that "Between 1830 and 1860 the nation was to put down more than 30,000 miles of railroad track" (180), and that, "By 1844 the machine had captured the public imagination. The invention of the steamboat had been exciting, but it was nothing compared to the railroad. . . . It is the embodiment of an age . . .—at once a testament to the will of man rising over

natural obstacles, and, yet, confined by its iron rails to a predetermined path, it suggests a new sort of fate" (191).

22. The area surrounding the Suspension Bridge, on the north side of Niagara Falls, was incorporated with the Village of Niagara Falls, formerly "Manchester," in 1892.

23. Hosfeld Smith, *Westward I Go Free*.

24. In *Westward I Go Free*, Hosfield Smith explains that the "two boxes of troches" Thoreau bought were "a popular throat lozenge. Newspapers of the day carried advertisements for Brown's Brochial Troches, which could cure "cough, cold, hoarseness, Influenza, any irritation," including bronchitis (94).

25. Thoreau's notes here are taken from a compilation of sources: *The First and Last Journeys of Thoreau: Lately Discovered among His Unpublished Journals and Manuscripts*, ed. Franklin Benjamin Sanborn (Boston, MA: printed exclusively for members of the Bibliophile Society, 1905). HathiTrust; *Thoreau's Minnesota Journey: Two Documents*, ed. Walter Harding (Geneseo, NY: Thoreau Society, 1962). HathiTrust; John R. Sligoe, *The Journal of Henry David Thoreau 1837–1861*, 659–60; and Corinne Hosfeld Smith, *Westward I Go Free: Tracing Thoreau's Last Journey*.

26. From *Life of Henry Wadsworth Longfellow: With Extracts from His Journals and Correspondence*, 2 vols., *1866 and 1867*, ed. Samuel Longfellow, 365.

27. *Life of Henry Wadsworth Longfellow*, 365.

28. Letter 1951, to Edith and Anne Allegra Longfellow, Niagara Falls, June 8, 1862. Reprint in *The Letters of Henry Wadsworth Longfellow*, vol. 4, *1857–1865*, ed. Samuel Longfellow.

29. *The Life of Henry Wadsworth*, 385–86.

Chapter 3

1. Thomas Moore, *Memoirs, Journal, and Correspondence of Thomas Moore*, ed. John Russell (London: Brown, Green, and Longmans, 1853).

2. Stephen Gwynn, *English Men of Letters: Thomas Moore* (London: Macmillan & Co., 1904).

3. Hawthorne quoted in James R. Mellow, *Nathaniel Hawthorne in His Times* (Baltimore, MD: Johns Hopkins University Press, 1998), 50.

4. This "Northern Tour" was, as Hawthorne biographer James R. Mellow puts it, "probably the most extensive he made during this period of his life. His travels can be reconstructed on only scanty documentary evidence: a letter written to his mother from Burlington, Vermont, in mid-September; a printed certification that Nathaniel Hawthorne had 'passed behind the Great Falling Sheet of Water to Termination Rock' at Niagara Falls, on September 28, 1832." *Nathaniel Hawthorne*, 51.

5. If American readers were interested in the developing identity of America—its landscape, language, literature and culture—those across the Atlantic were equally interested in critiquing it, and distinguishing its "British" neighbors just across the gorge. British travelers in the early decades of the new democracy were drawn to its shores, curious to know how this American "experiment" was unfolding. Tension almost immediately arose. For their part, the British tended to look down on American customs and manners, comparing their "infancy" and vulgarity to the long-established civilization of the Old World. Such condescension was evident in travel narratives by prominent British writers, most notably by Frances Trollope (*Domestic Manners of the Americans*, 1833), Anna Jameson (*Winter Studies and Summer Rambles in Canada*, 1838), and Charles Dickens (*American Notes for General Circulation*, 1842). British travelers often noted a feeling of relief once they stepped foot on "British" soil in Canada. A war of words developed as American writers sought to define a national identity.

6. The Frontier House was built in 1824 in Lewiston, New York. Though several writers likely stopped or stayed at the Frontier House, the lack of historical documents, such as a hotel register, make the claims difficult to verify.

7. Local historians working with the Niagara Falls Underground Railroad Heritage Center have documented black waiters working at the Cataract House Hotel from as early as 1840. See Judith Wellman. "Survey of Sites Relating to the Underground Railroad, Abolitionism, and African American Life in Niagara Falls and Surrounding Area, 1820–1880," the Niagara Falls Underground Railroad Heritage Area Management Plan, Appendix C. April 2012; Karolyn Smardz Frost, *Steal Away Home: One Woman's Epic Flight to Freedom and Her Long Road Back to the* South (Toronto, Canada: Harper Collins, 2017); and the Niagara Falls Underground Railroad Heritage Center.

8. "Home-spun" was an American idiom referring to clothes made for patriots during the Revolutionary War, refusing the use of British cloth. But by 1832, "home-spun cotton dress," may also be a reminder of what lay beyond this "Fashionable Tour": slavery. Travelling the Erie Canal, Hawthorne may have noted cotton mills in Utica, established as early as 1807, which could be glimpsed along the Canal. By 1810, there were 26 cotton mills in New York State. See H. H. Earl and F. M. Peck, "The Growth of the Cotton Industry in America," in *Fall River and Its Industries: History and Statistical Record* (New York: 1877). https://www.sailsinc.org/durfee/earl2.pdf. If Hawthorne was largely quiet on the topic of slavery, he did regard it as an evil, and his references, wittingly or not, are illustrative: the north was part of the economy that sustained slavery as an institution.

9. Biographer Richard Ellman notes of this quotation, that Wilde is "reputed to have said" this, but that "no contemporary account records it." *Oscar Wilde* (New York: Vintage Books, 1988), 160. The factuality of the quote is similarly questioned by David Friedman in *Wilde in America: Oscar Wilde and the Invention of Modern Celebrity* (New York: W. W. Norton, 2014), among others.

10. Wilde traveled to the US to promote the Gilbert and Sullivan opera *Patience* (1881), which was a satire of Aesthetes like Wilde who promoted art and artifice, and beauty over morality. But in his first lecture, "The English Renaissance," which he read at Buffalo, he outwits the critics, including Gilbert and Sullivan. "The true critic addresses not the artist ever," he said, "but the public."

11. As cited in Lloyd Lewis and Henry Justin Smith, *Oscar Wilde Discovers America [1882]* (New York: Harcourt, Brace, 1936), 163.

12. From "Impressions of America," 1883, in *The Collected Oscar Wilde*, edited by Angus Fletcher and George Stade (New York: Barnes & Noble Classics, 2007).

13. In their biography *Oscar Wilde Discovers America [1882]*, Lloyd Lewis and Henry Justin Smith make this interesting observation, however: "No one heard him mention those annoyances which had roused many another traveler to complain—the almost savage greed of hackmen; the exorbitant charges to see the sights; the numerous booths, shops, shell-games, gimcrack stores selling stuffed birds, gaudily colored glassware, and souvenirs; the avid photographers who sought to rope in travelers to be portrayed against a false cataract background" (162–63). Wilde's omission of the tourist "hacks" is unique in commentary on the Falls.

14. Qtd. in David M. Friedman, *Wilde in America*, 157–58.

15. Friedman makes this case for Wilde, for example in *Wilde in America*.

16. The park was designed by renowned landscape architect Frederick Law Olmsted, who, with Calvert Vaux, had previously designed Central Park in New York City. Olmsted wanted to create a natural environment around the Falls that would provide scenic settings for contemplation and rejuvenation.

17. "Wilde Sees the Falls," *Buffalo Express*, February 9, 1882; Repr. *Wheeling Register*, February 27, 1882, 3. Cited in Oscar Wilde, *Oscar Wilde in America: The Interviews*, ed. Matthew Hofer and Gary Scharnhorst (Urbana: University of Illinois Press, 2010).

Chapter 4

1. See, for example, Robert A. Gross, "Building a National Literature: The United States 1800–1890," in *A Companion to the History of the Book*, edited by Simon Eliot and Jonathan Rose (Malden, MA: Wiley-Blackwell, 2009), 315–28. Accessed November 15, 2019.

2. "Boz" was a pen-name of Dickens's. It was taken from his little brother's nickname "Moses," based on a character from a British novel, and which the younger Dickens sometimes mispronounced as "Boses." Dickens eventually shortened it to Boz.

3. "International Copyright," *New-York American*, Monday, May 9, 1842.

4. See Fuller entry in this collection for more on the "Jonathan" reference.

5. Dickens qtd. in Forster, 409. John Forster, *The Life of Charles Dickens*, vols. 1–3 (1875) (Boston, MA: James R. Osgood & Company). Accessed September 18, 2017.

6. "American Criticism on Dickens' Notes." *New York Herald*, Thursday, November 17, 1842; Issue 308.

7. Charles Dickens, "Preface," *American Notes* (1850), xi.

8. In "Washington Irving and Charles Dickens," scholar W. C. Desmond Pacey demonstrates that, "Irving's attitude toward Dickens did change. The decisive factor in this estrangement was not Dickens's alleged personal vulgarity, but his treatment of America and Americans in *American Notes* (1842) and *Martin Chuzzlewit* (1843). The fact that Irving's admiration for Dickens as a writer, and the memory of their happy associations in New York, Washington, and Baltimore, were outweighed by his desire to see America favorably pictured to the world" (337, 339). W. C. Desmond Pacey, "Washington Irving and Charles Dickens," *American Literature* 16, no. 4 (January 1945): 332–39.

9. Dickens was not as kind as these amendments suggest, as evidenced in private letters written to and published by John Forster. Though Dickens praised the Falls as before, even from the American side, he makes other criticisms, for instance on the attractiveness of women from Buffalo who attended his lectures. See Forster, *The Life of Charles Dickens*.

10. Like the Cataract House on the American side of the Falls, the Clifton House Hotel stood prominently over the Canadian gorge, where the current Oakes Garden Theatre stands, and also catered to the wealthy and well known.

11. Eugene, "Buffalo," *Weekly Herald*, Saturday, May 28, 1842, issue 36, 284. Gale Document Number: GT3004493037.

12. It should be noted that the Canadian side of the Falls does not escape Dickens's censure either. Here, he rants about the Table Rock registers, in which visitors recorded their impressions, often humorously or otherwise. Dickens boldly quotes a sign that requests that the musings should not be copied:

> On Table Rock there is a cottage belonging to a Guide, where little relics of the place are sold, and where visitors register their names in a book kept for the purpose. On the wall of the room in which a great many of these volumes are preserved, the following request is posted: "Visitors will please not copy nor extract the remarks and poetical effusions from the registers and albums kept here."

The irony was likely not lost on Dickens that his work was unprotected and reproduced at will, while the "vilest and the filthiest ribaldry that ever human hogs delighted in" was politely requested by the proprietor to be preserved as originals. It is possible that the book and the prohibition were too tempting for Dickens not to add his own comments. A published version of excerpts from the registers appeared in 1855 as *Table Rock Album*, containing an inscription by a writer who signed as "Boz." It is not possible to know whether this was *the* Boz, that is, Dickens, since the compilers of the *Album* do not present the entries in chronological order, thus no date is provided. Still, the sentiments the *Table Rock Album*'s "Boz." conveys about Niagara Falls are shared by the Boz of *American Notes*.

13. Though much of Twain's travel writing has received critical attention, little had been made of his "tours" of Niagara Falls until Thomas Reigstad's engaging book *Scribblin' for a Livin': Mark Twain's Pivotal Period in Buffalo* (Amherst, NY: Prometheus Books, 2013).

14. In *The Oxford Companion to Mark Twain*, Gregg Camfield notes, "While most historical theories of humor that were accepted during the 1800s agreed that humor arises from a perception of incongruity, the value of that perception was hotly contested." Twain himself at times worried over his use of a "low form" when he had high literary aspirations. See Gregg Camfield, *The Oxford Companion to Mark Twain* (Oxford: Oxford University Press, 2003), 275.

15. Twain later took Belford Brothers to court, in 1887, in *Clemens v. Belford*. Though Twain lost the case on the grounds that the publishers gave credit to the author by using his name, he hopefully had the last laugh when his 1906 statement on copyright to Congress helped to shape legislation in 1909, which protected works for fifty years after the author's death.

16. Gregg Camfield, *The Oxford Companion to Mark Twain*, 70.

17. Twain's comment is recorded in the *Louisville Post* when again facing issues of authorized rights to his work, this time over *Adventures of Huckleberry Finn* (qtd. in *Mark Twain: The Complete Interviews*. ("A Great Humorist" January 5, 1885, 1), 69.

18. "Mark Twain's Copyright: Why His Application Was Denied in Canada—Points of Canadian Law," *New York Times*, December 29, 1881.

19. Twain's reference is to Charles Blondin (born Jean-François Gravelet), the first tightrope walker, or "funambulist," to cross Niagara Falls on a high wire, which he first did on June 30, 1859. Blondin additionally, and famously, performed outrageous stunts on his many crossings.

Chapter 5

1. "An Act to Prevent the further Introduction of Slaves and to limit the Term of Contracts for Servitude Statutes of Upper Canada, 33. George III, Cap. 7, 1793." Archives of Ontario, http://www.archives.gov.on.ca/en/explore/online/alvin_mccurdy/big/big_03_anti_slavery_act.aspx. Accessed June 16, 2017.

2. John Sekora, "Is the Slave Narrative a Species of Autobiography?" in *Studies in Autobiography*, ed. James Olney (New York: Oxford University Press, 1988), 106.

3. Sekora explains: "Slaveowners possessed the increasingly elaborate state codes controlling the labor and physical being of slaves. Yet they sought more—

even the words, the very language of the slaves. To masters, the words of slaves appeared doubly significant. On the one hand, they were intimate, the personal expression of self and world. On the other, they were potent, lethal things." Sekora, "Black Message/White Envelope: Genre, Authenticity, and Authority in the Antebellum Slave Narrative," *Callaloo* 32 (Summer 1987): 485. Accessed June 13, 2017.

4. About this bearing witness, Charles T. Davis and Henry Louis Gates Jr. write in the edited collection *The Slave's Narrative* (1985): "The narrated, descriptive 'eye' was put into service as a literary form to posit both the individual 'I' of the black author, as well as the collective 'I' of the race" (xxvi). Sekora puts it thus: "Such recollection could then be united with other life stories to form a history, a time beyond personal memory, a time beyond slaveholders' power. The narrative is both instrument and inscription of a collective memory" (512).

5. Escaped slaves who could write their own autobiographies also found that the landscape, particularly Niagara, as symbol of a national identity, could be used to ironic effect. In his poem "Jefferson's Daughter" (1848), for instance, William Wells Brown, a fugitive living in Buffalo, New York, and assisting other enslaved people in their escape to freedom, questions the meaning of liberty if the former President of the United States Thomas Jefferson can both enslave and father those he would enslave. Niagara as symbol of power and freedom is meaningless in such an instance. "Can the tide of Niagara wipe out the stain?" asks Wells. To which he answers: "No! Jefferson's child has been bartered for gold!"

In an 1857 narrative, former slave Austin Steward, a Rochester, New York abolitionist similarly contrasts the natural sublimity of Niagara Falls to the inhumanity of the enslaver:

> How tame appear the works of art, and how insignificant the bearing of proud, puny man, compared with the awful grandeur of that natural curiosity. Yet there, the rich from all parts of the world, do congregate! There you will find the idle, swaggering slaveholder, blustering about in lordly style; boasting of his wealth; betting and gambling; ready to fight, if his slightest wish is not granted, and lavishing his cash on all who have the least claim upon him. Ah, well can he afford to be liberal,—well can he afford to spend thousands yearly at our Northern watering places; he has plenty of human chattels at home, toiling year after year for his benefit.

Austin Steward, *Twenty-two Years a Slave and Forty Years a Freeman* (Rochester, NY: William Alling, 1857).

6. Stowe's impressions are often cited in histories of Niagara Falls. Most notably, in *Imagining Niagara: The Meaning and Making of Niagara Falls* (Amherst: University of Massachusetts Press, 1994), Patrick McGreevy explores the themes of death and afterlife so evident in Stowe's passage. McGreevy offers several compelling explanations for Stowe's feeling that she "could have *gone over* with

the waters." In the nineteenth century, McGreevy notes, there existed "a fervid public discourse on the meaning of death" and the notion of an afterlife (42). Partly this discourse could be seen in the fascination with stories of death at the Falls in newspapers, guidebooks, and literature of the period that persist today. At the time of Stowe's visit, "as early as the 1830s," McGreevy notes, for example, "guidebooks repeated the gruesome details of accidents, suicides, murders, and narrow escapes" at the Falls (42). McGreevy points to museums of the *macabre* that accompany this fascination, such as those of Ripley's, Dracula, and Frankenstein on the Canadian side. But it was also the emblematic power and magnitude of the Falls that proved "a grim reminder of the ultimate limitedness of the human condition" (44).

7. Calvin Stowe's first wife, Eliza, close friend to Harriet Beecher, died while Harriet was on this trip east. Beecher and Stowe would marry in 1836.

8. The colonizationist view held that after emancipation, freed slaves should migrate to Africa, an ultimately racist approach to the question.

9. The Institute was founded by Stowe's sister Catherine Beecher.

10. Stowe's letter can be found in Annie Fields, ed. *Life and Letters of Harriet Beecher Stowe*, 1897. Facsimile reprint. Detroit: Gale Research Company, 1970, 89–90.

11. Fields, *Life and Letters*, 89.

12. Robin W. Winks, "The Making of a Fugitive Slave Narrative: Josiah Henson and Uncle Tom—A Case Study," in *The Slave's Narrative*, ed. Charles T. Davis and Henry Louis Gates Jr. (Oxford: Oxford University Press, 1985), 132, Ebrary. Accessed June 9, 2017.

Chapter 6

1. Estimates are taken from Daniel G. Hill, *The Freedom-Seekers: Blacks in Early Canada* (Agincourt, ON: Book Society of Canada Ltd., 1981). Questions have recently been raised over the Thirteenth Amendment due to this exception: "Neither slavery nor involuntary servitude, except as a punishment for crime whereof the party shall have been duly convicted, shall exist within the United States, or any place subject to their jurisdiction," which subsequently allowed for convict leasing and other injustices.

2. For more on the location of the first meeting, see, Cynthia Van Ness, "Buffalo Hotels and the Niagara Movement: New Evidence Refutes an Old Legend," *Western New York Heritage Magazine* 13, no. 4 (Winter 2011): 18–23.

3. Some accounts, like Sarah Bradford's, place the number of fugitives Tubman helped at around 300, but at least 70 can be confirmed.

4. Tubman was a member of the Salem Chapel, BME Church, which still stands in St. Catharines, Ontario.

5. For evidence of Harriet Tubman's journey over the Niagara Falls Suspension Bridge, see William H. Siener and Thomas A. Chambers. "Harriet Tubman and John A. Roebling's Niagara Suspension Bridge," *Western New York Heritage* (Spring 2010): 8–17. A pillar of the bridge still stands, across from the Niagara Falls Underground Railroad Heritage Center, New York.

6. Sarah H. Bradford, *Scenes in the Life of Harriet Tubman* (1869), and *The Moses of Her People* (Bedford, MA: Applewood Books, 1993), 35.

7. The Walt Whitman Archive provides these editorial notes on the journal entries: "This manuscript page consists of notes from Whitman's return trip from New Orleans in 1848. This page of notes, crossed out and numbered "2," describes the journey across Lake Erie; Whitman's visits to Buffalo, Albany, and Niagara Falls, and his arrival at Brooklyn. The notes were later used as the basis for an article titled "New Orleans in 1848" that appeared in the New Orleans Picayune on January 25, 1887. The article was reprinted in *November Boughs*." Walt Whitman, ["is rougher than it was"], the Walt Whitman Archive. Gen., ed. Ed Folsom and Kenneth M. Price, http://www.whitmanarchive.org. Accessed January 25, 2018.

8. "Starting from Paumanok" (1860), published in later edition of *Leaves of Grass, Leaves of Grass: First and "Death-Bed" Editions*, ed. Karen Karbiener (New York: Barnes and Noble, 2004), 11–12.

9. Walt Whitman, *Leaves of Grass: First and "Death-Bed" Editions*, l. 1–2, 5–6, 32).

10. In the summer of 1848, not long after his first visit to the Falls, Whitman returned to Western New York. On August 9 and 10, a biographer notes, he "attended the great antislavery convention held in Buffalo in early August. Along with some twenty thousand others, he heard many of the era's leading antislavery orators." Whitman shared a view with others at the Free Soil Convention that slavery should not extend to new western territories. David S. Reynolds *Walt Whitman* (Oxford, UK: Oxford University Press, 2005), 9. Whitman has recently come under critique for some of his representations of race, a debate that began in the 1950s. See, for example, Lavelle Porter, "Should Walt Whitman Be #Cancelled?" *JSTOR Daily*, April 17, 2019, https://daily.jstor.org/should-walt-whitman-be-cancelled/; *Whitman Noir: Black America and the Good Gray Poet*, ed. Ivy Wilson (Iowa City: University of Iowa Press, 2014); and Martin Klammer, "Whitman, Slavery, and the Emergence of *Leaves of Grass* (University Park: University of Pennsylvania Press, 1995).

11. See Walt Whitman, *The Correspondence of Walt Whitman, vol. 3: 1876–1885*, ed. Edwin Haviland Miller (New York: New York University Press, 1964).

Chapter 7

1. See Elizabeth McKinsey, *Niagara Falls: Icon of the American Sublime* (Cambridge: Cambridge University Press, 1985), 9–13. Kinsey notes that both

Hennepin and the artist wanted to convey the "idea" of the Falls and so drew on contemporary theories of landscape as well as symbolic and rhetorical devices to "wow" the reader.

2. James Russell Lowell and James T. Fields, who would, in 1866, offer Howells the assistant editor position.

3. Though at the hotel, Howells could have run into John Roebling, designer of the Suspension Bridge, and former senator and soon-to-be secretary of state, William Seward and his wife, who were also staying at the Cataract House at the time of Howells's visit.

4. Joseph Earl Arrington, "Godfrey N. Frankenstein's Moving Panorama of Niagara Falls," *New York History* 49, no. 2 (April 1968): 169.

5. Arrington, "Godfrey N. Frankenstein's Moving Panorama," 175.

6. Arrington, 178.

7. Susan Goodman and Carl Dawson. *William Dean Howells: A Writer's Life* (Berkeley: University of California Press, 2005), 174–76.

8. Howells usefully, though imperfectly here, quotes British poet Alfred, Lord Tennyson (1809–1892).

9. Morton Dauwen Zabel, ed., *The Art of Travel: Scenes and Journeys in America, England, France and Italy from the Travel Writings of Henry James* (Garden City, NJ: Doubleday Anchor Books, 1958), 36.

Chapter 8

1. In the early-nineteenth-century collection, *Sketches of Ancient History of the Six Nations* (1828), the Tuscarora author David Cusick, transcribes into English indigenous history and myth. Cusick writes that the alliance of the Five Nations was established, "Perhaps 1000 years before Columbus discovered the America" (22). Though historians have debated the establishment of the confederacy varying from 1100 to 1450, the latter mid-fifteenth-century date is generally suggested.

2. The "confederacy" is represented in the meaning of Haudenosaunee: "people who build a house" or "people of the long house."

3. The Hiawatha Belt represents the unity of the Haudenosaunee Confederacy among the original five nations, which was established before the Tuscarora arrived in the region in the eighteenth century, to constitute the Six Nations.

4. Quote taken from Arthur C. Parker, ed., *The Constitution of the Five Nations* (Albany: State University of New York Press, 1916).

5. Williams's quote can be found on p. 177 of his memoir.

6. Anthony Trollope's first impressions of the Falls appear in his travel book *The West Indies and the Spanish Main* (1860).

7. Frances Trollope also made a point to go to Niagara Falls in 1830. A visit to the Falls, she claimed, would make her travel book perfect. However, she had to borrow money get there.

8. John McCrae is from Ontario, Canada, where his house museum is located. His poem "In Flanders Fields," written during the Great War (the war that was to have ended all wars), has made the poppy flower a symbol of war remembrance: "In Flanders fields the poppies blow / Between the crosses, row on row."

9. The *Times*, April 26, 1915.

10. James Strachey, who may be most well known as having edited the complete volumes of Sigmund Freud, had loved Brooke, and the two exchanged a series of passionately romantic yet sometimes spiteful letters over the more than ten years they knew each other.

11. Now an obsolete term, the root word "ineffugible," according to the *Oxford English Dictionary*, means "inevitable."

Chapter 9

1. Definitions are taken from Donald Cazentre, *Spirits and Cocktails of Upstate New York: A History* (Charleston, SC: American Palate, 2017), 14–15.

2. James Fenimore Cooper, "Melancthon Taylor Woolsey," in *Sketches of Navy Men* (1839). Reprint, *Graham's Magazine* 26 (1845): 18.

3. Biographer Wayne Franklin notes that the 1847 trip, during which Cooper stopped to see Niagara Falls on his way home from Michigan, was the "first time since 1809." *James Fenimore Cooper: The Early Years* (New Haven: Yale University Press, 2007), 432.

4. Letter 1085. To William Branford Shubrick, written from Cooperstown, New York, July 22, 1850. Quoted in James Franklin Beard, ed., *The Letters and Journals of James Fenimore Cooper*, vol. 6: *1849–1851*, edited by James Franklin Beard (Cambridge, MA: Belknap, 1968), 206.

5. "Its Immensity," *Niagara Falls Gazette*, Monday, November 26, 1894.

6. Daniel Stashower, *Teller of Tales: The Life of Arthur Conan Doyle* (New York: Henry Holt, 1999), 305, 316.

7. Monday evening edition, July 3, 1922.

8. *Niagara Falls News Illustrated Niagara Falls and Its Industries*, 3. Niagara Falls Public Library.

9. A record of this prison sentence, with London's name included, can be found on Ancestry.com. *New York, Governor's Registers of Commitments to Prisons, 1842–1908*. Series A0603. Records of the Office of the Governor [New York State]. New York State Archives, Albany, New York.

10. See Tim Cresswell, *The Tramp in America*. London, UK: Reaktion Books, Limited, 2001.

Chapter 10

1. William Irwin, *The New Niagara: Tourism, Technology, and the Landscape of Niagara Falls, 1776–1917* (University Park: Pennsylvania State University Press, 1996), 94.

2. Wells quoted in Leon Edel and Gordon N. Ray, eds., *Henry James and H. G. Wells: A Record of the Friendship, Their Debate on the Arts of Fiction, and Their Quarrel* (Westport, CT: Greenwood Press, 1958), 107.

3. Oscar Wilde, "Impressions of America." (1883). *The Collected Oscar Wilde*, edited by Angus Fletcher and George Stade (New York: Barnes & Noble Classics, 2007), 295.

4. James quoted in *Henry James and H. G. Wells*, 115.

Epilogue

1. See Tim Cresswell, *Place: An Introduction* (Sussex: UK, Wiley Blackwell, 2015).

Works Cited

Angelo, Ray. "Thoreau as Botanist: An Appreciation and a Critique." *The Thoreau Quarterly* 45, no. 3 (1985): 15, 13–23.

Arrington, Joseph Earl. "Godfrey N. Frankenstein's Moving Panorama of Niagara Falls." *New York History* 49, no. 2 (April 1968): 169–99.

Atlantic Journal, and Friend of Knowledge, Vol. 1, nos. 1–8. Philadelphia: 1832–1833.

Berton, Pierre. *Niagara: A History of the Falls*. New York: Kodansha International, 1992.

Biron, Gerry. *The Cherished Curiosity: The Souvenir Beaded Bag in Historic Haudenosaunee (Iroquois Art)*. Brainerd, MN: Bang Printing, 2012.

Blake, David. *Walt Whitman and the Culture of American Celebrity*. New Haven, CT: Yale University Press, 2006.

Bowman, Peter James. *The Fortune Hunter: A German Prince in Regency England*. Luton, UK: Signal Books, 2011.

Boynton, Henry Walcott. *James Fenimore Cooper*. New York: Frederick Ungar, 1966.

Bradberry, Bill. "Black Menagerie: Home Again—Taking the Scenic Route" in *Niagara Falls Reporter* (July 23, 2002). http://niagarafallsreporter.com/menagerie59.html.

Bradford, Sarah H. *Harriet: The Moses of Her People* (1886). Bedford, MA: Applewood Books, 1993.

———. *Scenes in the Life of Harriet Tubman* (1869). Bedford, MA: Applewood Books, 1993.

Brown, William Wells. "Jefferson's Daughter." *The Anti-Slavery Harp*. Boston: Bela Marsh, 1848.

Bruchac, Joseph. "Being Iroquois: Arthur C. Parker." *Voices: The Journal of New York Folklore* 41 (Spring–Summer 2015).

"Buffalo, Eugene." *Weekly Herald* 36 (May 28, 1842): 284. Gale Document Number: GT3004493037.

Burstein, Andrew. *The Original Knickerbocker: The Life of Washington Irving*. New York: Basic Books, 2007.

Camfield, Gregg. *The Oxford Companion to Mark Twain*. Oxford, UK: Oxford University Press, 2003.

Campbell, Killis. "The Kennedy Papers: A Sheaf of Unpublished Letters from Washington Irving." *The Sewanee Review* 25, no. 1 (January 1917): 1–19.

Cazentre, Donald. *Spirits and Cocktails of Upstate New York: A History*. Charleston, SC: American Palate, 2017.

Chevigny, Bell Gale. *The Woman and the Myth: Margaret Fuller's Life and Writings*. Old Westbury, NY: The Feminist Press, 1976.

Cmiel, Kenneth. "'A Broad Fluid Language of Democracy': Discovering the American Idiom." In *Discovering America: Essays on the Search for Identity*, edited by David Thelen and Frederick E. Hoxie. Urbana: University of Illinois Press, 1994.

Conrad, Peter. *Imagining America*. New York: Oxford University Press, 1980.

Cooper, James Fenimore. *The Letters and Journals of James Fenimore Cooper*. Vol. 5, *1845–1859*, edited by James Franklin Beard. Cambridge, MA: Belknap, 1968.

———. *The Letters and Journals of James Fenimore Cooper*. Vol. 6, *1849–1851*, edited by James Franklin Beard. Cambridge, MA: Belknap, 1968.

———. "Melancthon Taylor Woolsey." From *Sketches of Navy Men* (1839). *Graham's Magazine* 26 (1845): 14–21.

———. *The Spy; A Tale of Neutral Ground* (1821).

Cooper, John. "Home Page." Oscar Wilde in America. Accessed May–June 2016. http://www.oscarwildeinamerica.org/.

Cresswell, Tim. *Place: An Introduction*. Sussex: Wiley Blackwell, 2015.

———. *The Tramp in America*. London: Reaktion Books, 2001.

Cusick, David. *David Cusick's Sketches of Ancient History of the Six Nations*, edited by Paul Royster. Lincoln, NE: Faculty Publications, UNL Libraries, 1828. 24. https://digitalcommons.unl.edu/libraryscience/24.

Daily National Journal, no. 887 (July 7, 1827). Gale Document Number: GT3012498261.

Damon-Bach, Lucinda L., and Victoria Clements, eds. *Catharine Maria Sedgwick: Critical Perspectives*. Boston, MA: Northeastern University Press, 2003.

Dann, Kevin. *Expect Great Things: The Life and Search of Henry David Thoreau*. New York: TarcherPerigree, 2017.

Davis, Charles T., and Henry Louis Gates Jr., eds. *The Slave's Narrative*. Oxford: Oxford University Press, 1985.

Demos, John. *The Unredeemed Captive: A Family Story from Early America*. New York: Vintage Books, 1994.

DeVeaux, Samuel. *The Traveller's Own Book, to Saratoga Springs, Niagara Falls and Canada*. Buffalo, NY: Faxon & Co., 1841.

Dickens, Charles. *American Notes*. London: Chapman & Hall, 1842.

"Dickens's Notes." Editorial. *Scioto Gazette-Ohio*, November 24, 1842, 33. Gale Document Number: GT3009773389.

Documenting the American South. Webpage. University of North Carolina at Chapel Hill. http://docsouth.unc.edu.

Dow, Charles Mason. *Anthology and Bibliography of Niagara Falls*. Vols. 1 and 2. Albany, NY: J. B. Lyon, 1921.

Doyle, Arthur Conan. *Our American Adventure*. New York: George H. Doran Co., 1923.

Dubinsky, Karen. *The Second Greatest Disappointment: Honeymooning and Tourism at Niagara Falls*. New Brunswick, NJ: Rutgers University Press, 1999.

Earl, H. H., and F. M. Peck. "The Growth of the Cotton Industry in America." In *Fall River and Its Industries: History and Statistical Record*. New York: 1877. https://www.sailsinc.org/durfee/earl2.pdf.

Edel, Leon. *Henry James: A Life*. New York: Harper & Row, 1985.

Edel, Leon, and Gordon N. Ray. *Henry James and H.G. Wells: A Record of the Friendship, Their Debate on the Arts of Fiction, and Their Quarrel*, edited by Leon Edel. Westport, CT: Greenwood Press, 1958.

Ellman, Richard. *Oscar Wilde*. New York: Vintage Books, 1988.

Emerson, Ralph Waldo. *The Letters of Ralph Waldo Emerson*. Vol. 3, *1842–1847*, edited by Ralph L. Rusk. New York: Columbia University Press, 1939.

———. *The Letters of Ralph Waldo Emerson*. Vol. 4, *1848–1855*, edited by Ralph L. Rusk. New York: Columbia University Press, 1939.

———. *The Letters of Ralph Waldo Emerson*. Vol. 5, *1856–1867*, edited by Ralph L. Rusk. New York: Columbia University Press, 1939.

———. *The Letters of Ralph Waldo Emerson*. Vol. 6, *1868–1881*, edited by Ralph L. Rusk. New York: Columbia University Press, 1939.

———. *The Journals and Miscellaneous Notebooks of Ralph Waldo Emerson*. Vol. 11, *1848–1851*, edited by A. W. Plumstead, William H. Gilman, and Ruth H. Bennett. Cambridge, MA: Belknap Press, 1975.

———. *The Journals and Miscellaneous Notebooks of Ralph Waldo Emerson*. Vol. 14, *1854–1861*, edited by Susan Sutton Smith and Harrison Hayford. Cambridge, MA: Belknap Press, 1978.

———. *The Journals and Miscellaneous Notebooks of Ralph Waldo Emerson*. Vol. 15, *1860–1866*, edited by Linda Allardt and David W. Hill. Cambridge, MA: Belknap Press, 1982.

———. *The Journals and Miscellaneous Notebooks of Ralph Waldo Emerson*. Vol. 16, edited by Ronald A. Bosco and Glen M. Johnson, 411 and 417. Cambridge, MA: Belknap Press, 1982.

57th Annual Report of the Regents of the University, to the Legislature of the State of New York. Albany: University of the State of New York. Board of Regents, 1844.

Fagant, John. "The Free Soil Party Convention in Buffalo, August 9 & 10, 1848." Buffalo Architecture and History. Accessed January 26, 2018. buffaloah.com/h/free.pdf.

Ferris, Theodore. "One Dickens of a Time: Charles Dickens Visits the Great Lakes Region." *Island Seas, Quarterly Journal of the Great Lakes Historical Society* 35, no. 4 (Winter 1979): 269–75.

Fields, Annie, ed. *Life and Letters of Harriet Beecher Stowe* (1897). Facsimile reprint. Detroit: Gale Research Company, 1970.

Folsom, Ed, and Kenneth M. Price, eds. ["is rougher than it was]." The Walt Whitman Archive. Accessed January 25, 2018. http://www.whitmanarchive.org.

Forster, John, ed. *The Life of Charles Dickens*. 3 vols. London: Chapman and Hall, 1872–1874.

Franklin, Wayne, and Michael Steiner. "Taking Place: Toward the Regrounding of American Studies," 3. In *Mapping American Culture*, edited by Wayne Franklin and Michael Steiner. Iowa City: University of Iowa Press, 1992.

Franklin, Wayne. *James Fenimore Cooper: The Early Years*. New Haven, CT: Yale University Press, 2007.

Fraser, Robert L. "William Forsyth." In *Provincial Justice: Upper Canadian Legal Portraits from the Dictionary of Canadian Biography*, edited by Robert L. Fraser. Toronto: University of Toronto Press, 1992.

Friedman, David M. *Wilde in America: Oscar Wilde and the Invention of Modern Celebrity*. New York: W. W. Norton, 2014.

Frost, Karolyn Smardz. *Steal Away Home: One Woman's Epic Flight to Freedom and Her Long Road Back to the South*. Toronto, Canada: Harper Collins, 2017.

Fuller, Margaret. *The Letters of Margaret Fuller*. Vol. 3, *1842–44*, edited by Robert N. Hudspeth. Ithaca, NY: Cornell University Press, 1984.

———. *Summer on the Lakes, in 1843* (1844) Repr. *The Portable Margaret Fuller*. New York: Penguin, 1994.

Gassan, Richard H. *The Birth of American Tourism: New York, the Hudson Valley, and American Culture, 1790–1835*. Amherst: University of Massachusetts Press, 2008.

———. "The First American Tourist Guidebooks: Authorship and the Print Culture of the 1820s." *Book History* 8 (2005): 51–74.

Glendenning, Victoria. *Anthony Trollope*. New York: Alfred A. Knopf, 1993.

Goodman, Susan, and Carl Dawson. *William Dean Howells: A Writer's Life*. Berkeley: University of California Press, 2005.

Goodrich, S. G. *A System of Universal Geography, Popular and Scientific: Comprising a Physical, Political and Statistical Account of the World and Its Various Divisions*. Philadelphia, PA: Key, Mielke & Biddle, 1832.

Gordon, Beverly. "Souvenirs of Niagara Falls: The Significance of Indian Whimsies." *New York History* 67, no. 4 (October 1986): 389–409.

Grant, John, and Ray Jones. *Niagara Falls: An Intimate Portrait*. Guilford, CT: Insider's Guide, 2006.

Grimes, William. *Straight Up or On the Rocks: The Story of the American Cocktail*. New York: North Point Press, 2001.

Gross, Robert A. "Building a National Literature: The United States 1800–1890." In *A Companion to the History of the Book*, edited by Simon Eliot and Jonathan Rose. Malden, MA: Wiley-Blackwell, 2009. 315–28.

Guthrie, John, and the Niagara Falls Public Library. "The Niagara Falls Historical Photograph Collection." Niagara Falls Thunder Alley. Accessed June 18, 2018. http://www.niagarafrontier.com/tashapageone.html.

Gwynn, Stephen. *English Men of Letters: Thomas Moore*. London: Macmillan, 1904.

Haigh, Ted. "The Origin of the Cocktail." *Imbibe*. February 24, 2009. http://imbibemagazine.com/origin-of-the-cocktail.

———. *Vintage Spirits and Forgotten Cocktails*. Beverly, MA: Quarry Books, 2009.

Hallett, Adam. "Made of the Mist: Nineteenth-Century British and American Views of Niagara, 1." *Literature Compass* 1, no. 3 (2014): 159–72.

———. "Made of the Mist: Nineteenth-Century British and American Views of Niagara, 2." *Literature Compass* 1, no. 3 (2014): 173–89.

Hall, N. John. *Trollope: A Biography*. Oxford: Clarendon Press, 1991.

Harris, Jennifer, and Hilary Iris Lowe. *From Page to Place: American Literary Tourism and the Afterlives of Authors*. Amherst: University of Massachusetts Press, 2017.

Hassan, Richard H. *The Birth of American Tourism: New York, the Hudson Valley, and American Culture, 1790–1835*. Amherst: University of Massachusetts Press, 2008.

Hawthorne, Nathaniel. "The Canal Boat." (1835) *Mosses from an Old Manse*. Boston: Houghton Mifflin, 1882.

———. "My Visit to Niagara." (1835) *The Works of Nathaniel Hawthorne*. Vol. 12, edited by George Parsons Lathrop. St. Clair Shores, MI: Scholarly Press, 1891.

Hedrick, Joan D. *Harriet Beecher Stowe: A Life*. New York: Oxford University Press, 1994.

Hennepin, Louis. *A New Discovery of a Vast Country in America* (1698) Chicago: A. C. McClurg, 1903.

Hennessy, James Pope. *Anthony Trollope*. Boston, MA: Little, Brown, 1971.

Henson, Josiah. *The Life of Josiah Henson, Formerly a Slave, Now an Inhabitant of Canada, as Narrated by Himself*. Boston: Arthur D. Phelps, 1849.

Hill, Daniel G. *The Freedom-Seekers: Blacks in Early Canada*. Agincourt, Canada: Book Society of Canada, 1981.

Hodge, Francis. *Yankee Theatre: The Image of America on the Stage, 1825–1850*. Austin: University of Texas Press, 1964.

Hofer, Matthew, and Gary Scharhorst, eds. *Oscar Wilde in America: The Interviews*. Urbana: University of Illinois Press, 2010.

Holley, George Washington. *The Falls of Niagara and Other Famous Cataracts*. London: Hodder and Stoughton, 1882.

———. *Niagara: Its 1872 History and Geology, Incidents and Poetry*. Buffalo, NY, 1872.

Homes of American Authors; Comprising Anecdotal, Personal, and Descriptive Sketches by Various Writers. New York: G. P. Putnam, 1853.

Hoppen, Anne, Lorrain Brown, and Alan Fyall. "Literary Tourism: Opportunities and Challenges for the Marketing and Branding of Destinations?" *Journal of Destination Marketing & Management* 3 (2014): 37–47.

Howells, William Dean. "En Passant." Ohio Memory. Ohio History Connection, July 24, 1860. http://www.ohiomemory.org.

Hulett, T. G. *Every Man His Own Guide to the Falls of Niagara: Or the Whole Story in a Few Words*. Buffalo, NY: Faxon & Read, 1842.

Humez, Jean M. *Harriet Tubman: The Life and the Life Stories*. Madison: The University of Wisconsin Press, 2003.

Illustrated Niagara Falls and Its Industries. Niagara Falls News. Special Souvenir Number. Niagara Falls, NY: Power City Publishing Company, 1907. Niagara Falls Public Library.

Immortal Niagara. Chamber of Commerce. Niagara Falls, NY: Power City Press, 1941.

Irving, Pierre M. *The Life and Letters of Washington Irving*. Vol. 1. New York: Putnam, 1864. Republished Detroit, MI: Gale Research, 1967.

Irving, Washington. *Washington Irving Journals and Notebooks*. Vol. 5, *1832–1859*, edited by Sue Fields Ross. Boston: Twayne, 1986.

———. *Washington Irving Letters*. Vol. 2, *1823–1838*, edited by Ralph M. Aderman, Herbert L. Kleinfield, and Jenifer S. Banks. Boston: Twayne, 1979.

Irwin, William. *The New Niagara: Tourism, Technology, and the Landscape of Niagara Falls, 1776–1917*. University Park: Pennsylvania State University Press, 1996.

Jackson, John N. *The Mighty Niagara: One River—Two Frontiers*. Amherst, NY: Prometheus, 2003.

James, Henry. "Niagara." *The Nation*. October 12–19, 1871.

Jameson, Anna. *Winter Studies and Summer Rambles*. London: Saunders and Otley, 1838.

Kershaw, Alex. *Jack London: A Life*. New York: St. Martin's Griffin, 1997.

Ketterer, David. "Mark Twain's Overlooked 'Second Speech' in Montreal." *Mark Twain Journal* 28, no. 2 (Fall 1990): 21–23.

Killingsworth, M. Jimmie. *Walt Whitman and the Earth: A Study in Ecopoetics*. Iowa City: University of Iowa Press, 2004.

Klammer, Martin. *Whitman, Slavery, and the Emergence of Leaves of Grass*. University Park: University of Pennsylvania Press, 1995.

Konkle, Maureen. *Writing Indian Nations: Native Intellectuals and the Politics of Historiography, 1827–1863*. Chapel Hill: University of North Carolina Press, 2004.

Kostoff, Bob. *Remembering Niagara: Tales from Beyond the Falls*. Charleston, SC: The History Press, 2008.

Larkin, Janet Dorothy. *Overcoming Niagara: Canals, Commerce, and Tourism in the Niagara-Great Lakes Borderland Region, 1792–1837*. Albany: State University of New York Press, 2018.
Laurie, Margaret S. *Lewiston: Crown Jewel of the Niagara*. Niagara Falls, NY: The Book Corner, 2001.
Lewis, Lloyd and Henry Justin Smith. *Oscar Wilde Discovers America [1882]*. NY: Harcourt, Brace, and Co., 1936. Print.
LeMaster, J. R., and Donald D. Kummings, eds. *The Routledge Encyclopedia of Walt Whitman*. New York: Routledge, 1998.
LeMaster, J. R., and James D. Wilson. *The Mark Twain Encyclopedia*. New York: Garland Publishing, 1993.
London, Jack. *The Road*. New York: Macmillan, 1907.
Longfellow, Henry Wadsworth. *The Letters of Henry Wadsworth Longfellow*. Vol. 4, *1857–1865*, edited by Andrew Hilen. Cambridge, MA: Belknap Press, 1972.
———. *Life of Henry Wadsworth Longfellow: With Extracts from His Journals and Correspondence,* edited by Samuel Longfellow. 2 vols. Boston, MA: Boston, Ticknor, 1886 and 1887.
Lynch, Tom, Cheryll Glotfelty, and Karla Armbruster. *Bioregional Imagination: Literature, Ecology, and Place*. Athens: University of Georgia Press, 2012.
"Mark Twain's Copyright: Why His Application Was Denied in Canada—Points of Canadian Law." *New York Times*, December 29, 1881.
Marshall, Megan. *Margaret Fuller: A New American Life*. Boston: Mariner Books, 2013.
Marx, Leo. *The Machine in the Garden* (1964). New York: Oxford University Press, 2000.
Matteson, John. *The Lives of Margaret Fuller: A Biography*. New York: W. W. Norton, 2012.
McGavran Murray, Meg. *Margaret Fuller: Wandering Pilgrim*. Athens: University of Georgia Press, 2008.
McGreevy, Patrick. *Imagining Niagara: The Meaning and Making of Niagara Falls*. Amherst: University of Massachusetts Press, 1994.
McKinsey, Elizabeth. *Niagara Falls: Icon of the American Sublime*. Cambridge: Cambridge University Press, 1985.
Mellow, James R. *Nathaniel Hawthorne in His Times*. Baltimore, MD: Johns Hopkins University Press, 1998.
Ministry of Government and Consumer Services. "An Act to Prevent the further Introduction of Slaves and to Limit the Term of Contracts for Servitude Statutes of Upper Canada Cap. 7, 33 George III, 1793." Archives of Ontario. Accessed June 16, 2017. http://www.archives.gov.on.ca/en/explore/online/alvin_mccurdy/big/big_03_anti_slavery_act.aspx.

The Monthly Repository, and Library of Entertaining Knowledge. Vols. 3.4 and 3.6. New York: Francis S. Wiggins, 1832.

Moore, Thomas. *Thomas Moore, the Poet: His Life and Works*, edited by Andrew James Symington. New York: Harper and Brothers, 1880.

Morgan, Winifred. *An American Icon: Brother Jonathan and American Identity*. Newark: University of Delaware Press, 1988.

Mulvey, Christopher. "New York to Niagara by Way of the Hudson and the Erie." In *The Cambridge Companion to American Travel Writing*, edited by Alfred Bendixen and Judith Hamera, 46–61. Cambridge: Cambridge University Press, 2009.

Nast, Thomas. *Innocence Abroad in Search of a Copyright/Th. Nast*. Photograph. The Library of Congress. Accessed July 12, 2017. https://www.loc.gov/item/2013650190/.

Nelson, Velvet. *An Introduction to the Geography of Tourism*. Lanham, MD: Rowman and Littlefield, 2013.

Niagara Falls USA. "Niagara Falls USA Seeing Record Visitation Numbers." Webpage. Accessed July 22, 2015. http://www.niagara-usa.com/articles/view/niagara-falls-usa-seeing-record-visitation-numbers/767/#.V0XH0nAnJNJ.

———. "Niagara Tourism and Convention Corporation Annual Report 2014." Webpage. Accessed May 25, 2016. http://www.niagara-usa.com.

Niagara Gazette (January 7, 1863): no. 454, roll #12, *NF Gazette*–Weekly, January 7, 1863–December 30, 1863. Niagara Falls Public Library.

Nichols, Wallace J. *Blue Mind: The Surprising Science That Shows How Being Near, In, or Under Water Can Make You Happier, Healthier, More Connected, and Better at What You Do*. New York: Little, Brown and Company, 2014.

Nye, David E. *Narratives and Spaces: Technology and the Construction of American Culture*. New York: Columbia University Press, 1997.

Olsen, Rodney D. *Dancing In Chains: The Youth of William Dean Howells*. New York: New York University Press, 1991.

Olney, James. "'I Was Born': Slave Narratives, Their Status as Autobiography and as Literature." *Callaloo* 20 (Winter 1984): 46–73.

Osborne, John B. "Preparing for the Pandemic: City Boards of Health and the Arrival of Cholera in Montreal, New York, and Philadelphia in 1832." *Urban History Review/Revue d'histoire urbaine* 36, no. 2 (Spring 2008): 29–42.

Oxford English Dictionary. 2nd ed. Vol. 7. Oxford: Clarendon, 1989.

Pacey, W. C. Desmond. "American Literature: Washington Irving and Charles Dickens." *American Literature* 16, no. 4 (January 1945): 332–39.

Parker, Arthur C., ed. *The Constitution of the Five Nations*. Albany: University of the State of New York, 1916.

———. "The Stone Giant's Battle." *Seneca Myths and Folktales*. Buffalo, NY: Buffalo Historical Society, 1923.

Patricia, Jasen. *Wild Things: Nature, Culture, and Tourism in Ontario, 1790–1914*. Toronto: University of Toronto Press, 2000.

Pindell, Richard. "Off to Niagara Falls: Charles Dickens' First American Tour." *Historic Traveler*, March/April 1995.

Porter, Lavelle. "Should Walt Whitman Be #Cancelled?" *JSTOR Daily*, April 17, 2019. Accessed August 16, 2019. https://daily.jstor.org/should-walt-whitman-be-cancelled/.

Porter, Peter A. Poem, in *Niagara: Its 1872 History and Geology, Incidents and Poetry*, edited by George Washington Holley. Buffalo, NY, 1872.

Price, Robert, ed. "The Road to Boston: 1860 Travel Correspondence of William Dean Howells." *Ohio History Journal* 80 (Spring 1971): 85–154. Accessed August 5, 2018. http://resources.ohiohistory.org/ohj/browse/displaypages.php?display=0080&display=85&display=154.

Pyle, G. F. "The Diffusion of Cholera in the United States in the Nineteenth Century." *Geographical Analysis* 1, no. 1 (January 1969): 59–75.

Radus, Daniel M. "Printing Native History in David Cusick's *Sketches of Ancient History of the Six Nations*." *American Literature* 86, no. 2 (June 2014): 217–43.

Redmond, Christopher. *Welcome to America, Mr. Sherlock Holmes: Victorian America Meets Arthur Conan Doyle*. Toronto: Simon & Pierre, 1987.

Reigstad, Thomas. J. *Scribblin' for a Livin': Mark Twain's Period in Buffalo*. Amherst, NY: Prometheus Books, 2013.

Revie, Linda L. *The Niagara Companion: Explorers, Artists, and Writers at the Falls, from Discovery through the Twentieth Century*. Ontario, Canada: Wilfrid Laurier University Press, 2003.

Reynolds, David S. *Walt Whitman*. Oxford: Oxford University Press, 2005.

Roe, Nicholas. *Romanticism: An Oxford Guide*. Oxford: Oxford University Press, 2005.

Roper, Gordon. "Mark Twain and His Canadian Publishers: A Second Look." *Papers of the Bibliographical Society of Canada* 5, no. 1. Accessed July 20, 2017.

Rosenberg, Charles E. *The Cholera Years: The United States in 1832, 1849, and 1866*. Chicago, IL: University of Chicago Press, 1987.

Ross, Sue Fields, ed. *Washington Irving: Journals and Notebooks*. Vol. 5, *1832–1859*. Boston, MA: Twayne Publishers, 1986.

Round, Phillip H. *Removable Type: Histories of the Book in Indian Country, 1663–1880*. Chapel Hill: University of North Carolina Press, 2010.

Rusk, Ralph K. *The Life of Ralph Waldo Emerson*. New York: Scribner's Sons, 1949.

"Save Niagara." *Goodwin's Weekly: A Thinking Paper for Thinking People* (July 28, 1906).

Sedgwick, Catharine Maria. *Life and Letters of Catharine M. Sedgwick*, edited by Mary Dewey. New York: Harper, 1871.

———. "The Catholic Iroquois." *Sedgwick Stories: The Periodical Writings of Catharine Maria Sedgwick*. Accessed July 24, 2018. https://sedgwickstories.omeka.net/items/show/32.

Sekora, John. "Black Message/White Envelope: Genre, Authenticity, and Authority in the Antebellum Slave Narrative." *Callaloo* 32 (Summer 1987): 482–515.

———. "Is the Slave Narrative a Species of Autobiography?" In *Studies in Autobiography*, edited by James Olney, 99–111. New York: Oxford University Press, 1988.

Sernett, Milton C. *North Star Country: Upstate New York and the Crusade for African American Freedom*. Syracuse, NY: Syracuse University Press, 2002.

Shaw, Ronald E. *Erie Water West: A History of the Erie Canal, 1792–1854*. Lexington, KY: University of Kentucky Press, 1966.

Sherborne, Michael. *H. G. Wells: Another Kind of Life*. London: Peter Owen, 2010.

Siener, William H., and Thomas A. Chambers. "Crossing to Freedom: Harriet Tubman and John A. Roebling's Suspension Bridge." In *Western New York Heritage Magazine*. New York: Western New York Heritage Press, 2010.

Sigourney, Lydia. "Niagara." *Monitor: Conducted by a Committee of the Union Ministerial Association*. October 8, 1834.

Smith, Corinne Hosfeld. "Notes on the Journey West." Transcription. The Huntington Library, San Marino, CA.

———. *Westward I Go Free: Tracing Thoreau's Last Journey*. Faringdon, UK: Green Frigate Books, 2012.

Speake, Jennifer. *Literature of Travel and Exploration: an Encyclopedia*. Vol. 1. New York: Fitzroy Dearborn, 2003.

Stashower, Arthur. *Teller of Tales: The Life of Arthur Conan Doyle*. New York: Henry Holt, 1999.

Steele, Jeffrey, ed. *The Essential Margaret Fuller*. New Brunswick, NJ: Rutgers University Press, 1992.

Steward, Austin. *Twenty-two Years a Slave and Forty Years a Freeman*. Rochester, New York: William Alling, 1857.

Stowe, Harriet Beecher. *The Key to Uncle Tom's Cabin*. New York: Arno Press and The New York Times, 1968.

Stowe, William W. "'Property in the Horizon': Landscape and American Travel Writing." In *The Cambridge Companion to American Travel Writing*, edited by Alfred Bendixen and Judith Hamera. Cambridge: Cambridge University Press, 2009.

Strand, Ginger. *Inventing Niagara: Beauty, Power, and Lies*. New York: Simon & Shuster, 2008.

Sturtevant, William C. "David and Dennis Cusick: Early Iroquois Realist Artists." *American Indian Art Magazine* (2006). Smithsonian Research Online. Accessed November 30, 2019. https://repository.si.edu/handle/10088/31964.

Symington, Andrew James. *Thomas Moore, the Poet: His Life and Works*. New York: Harper and Brothers, 1880.

Szlezák, Klara Stephanie. "Sages and Souvenirs: The Origins of American Literary Tourism in Concord, Massachusetts." In *Literature and Consumption in Nineteenth-Century America*, edited by Nicole Maruo-Schröder and Christoph Ribbat. Heidelberg: Universitätsverlag Winter, 2014.

Table Rock Album and Sketches of the Falls and Scenery Adjacent. Buffalo, New York: Thomas & Lathrops, 1855.

Thomas, Owen. *Niagara's Freedom Trail: A Guide to African-Canadian History on the Niagara Peninsula.* Niagara Falls, Canada: Niagara Economic and Tourism Corporation, 1996.

Thoreau, Henry David. *The Correspondence of Henry David Thoreau*, edited by Walter Harding and Carl Bode. New York: New York University Press, 1958.

———. *The First and Last Journeys of Thoreau: Lately Discovered among His Unpublished Journals and Manuscripts*, edited by Franklin Benjamin Sanborn. Boston: Bibliophile Society, 1905.

———. *The Journal: 1837–1861*, edited by Damion Searls. New York: New York Review Books, 2009.

———. *Thoreau's Minnesota Journey: Two Documents*, edited by Walter Harding. Geneseo, NY: Thoreau Society, 1962.

Tobin, Jacqueline. *From Midnight to Dawn: The Last Tracks of the Underground Railroad.* New York: Doubleday, 2007.

Trollope, Anthony. *North America* (1862) London: Chapman and Hall, 1866.

Trubek, Anne. *A Skeptic's Guide to Writers' Houses.* Philadelphia: University of Pennsylvania Press, 2011.

Tuite, Ashleigh R., Christina H. Chan, and David N. Fisman. "Cholera, Canals, and Contagion: Rediscovering Dr. Beck's Report." *Journal of Public Health Policy* 32, no. 3: 320–33.

Twain, Mark [Samuel Clemens]. *Buffalo Express* (Buffalo, NY), 1866–1878. August 21, 1869, 1, image 1. Image provided by Buffalo History Museum. Accessed July 20, 2017. http://nyshistoricnewspapers.org/lccn/sn83030921/1869-08-21/ed-1/seq-1/.

———. *Following the Equator.* Hartford, Connecticut: American Pub. Co., 1897.

———. *Mark Twain at the Buffalo Express*, edited by Joseph B. McCullough and Janice McIntire-Strasburg. DeKalb: Northern Illinois University, 2000.

———. *Mark Twain: The Complete Interviews*, edited by Gary Scharnhorst. Tuscaloosa: University of Alabama Press, 2006.

Van Ness, Cynthia. "Buffalo Hotels and the Niagara Movement: New Evidence Refutes an Old Legend." *Western New York Heritage* 13, no. 4 (Winter 2011): 18–23.

Vanderhaar Allen, Margaret. *The Achievement of Margaret Fuller.* University Park: Pennsylvania State University Press, 1979.

Vogel, Michael N. *Echoes in the Mist: An Illustrated History of the Niagara Falls Area.* Chatsworth, CA: Windsor Publications, 1991.

von Mehren, Joan. *Minerva and the Muse: A Life of Margaret Fuller.* Amherst, MA: University of Massachusetts Press, 1994.

Walls, Laura Dassow. *Henry David Thoreau: A Life.* Chicago, IL: University of Chicago Press, 2017.

Weber, Alfred, Beth L. Lueck, and Dennis Berthold. *Hawthorne's American Travel Sketches*. Hanover, NH: University Press of New England, 1989.

Weierman, Karen Woods. *One Nation, One Blood: Interracial Marriage in American Fiction, Scandal, and Law, 1820–1870*. Amherst, MA: University of Massachusetts Press, 2005.

———. "Reading and Writing 'Hope Leslie': Catherine Maria Sedgwick's Indian 'Connections.'" *New England Quarterly* 75, no. 3 (September 2002): 415–43. https://www.jstor.org/stable/1559786.

Weinstein, Cindy. "Introduction." *The Cambridge Companion to Harriet Beecher Stowe*, edited by Cindy Weinstein. Cambridge: Cambridge University Press, 2004.

Wellman, Judith. "Survey of Sites Relating to the Underground Railroad, Abolitionism, and African American Life in Niagara Falls and Surrounding Area, 1820–1880," The Niagara Falls Underground Railroad Heritage Area Management Plan, Appendix C, April 2012.

Wells, H. G. "The End of Niagara." *Harper's Weekly* L, no. 2587 (Saturday, July 21, 1906).

Whitman, Walt. *The Correspondence of Walt Whitman*. Vol. III: *1876–1885*, edited by Edwin Haviland Miller. New York: New York University Press, 1964.

———. *Daybooks & Notebooks*. Vol. 1: *1876–1881*, edited by Willie White. New York: New York University Press, 1978.

———. "[is rougher than it was]." The Walt Whitman Archive, edited by Ed Folsom and Kenneth M. Price. Accessed January 25, 2018. http://www.whitmanarchive.org.

———. *Leaves of Grass. First and "Death-Bed" Editions*, edited by Karen Karbiener. New York: Barnes and Noble, 2004.

Wilde, Oscar. "Impressions of America." (1883). *The Collected Oscar Wilde*, edited by Angus Fletcher and George Stade. New York: Barnes & Noble Classics, 2007.

———. "The English Renaissance." (1882 Lecture). *The Collected Oscar Wilde*, edited by Angus Fletcher and George Stade. New York: Barnes & Noble Classics 2007.

Williams, Stanley T. *The Life of Washington Irving*. Vol. 2. New York: Oxford University Press, 1935.

Williams, Ted. "The Great Law of the Great Peace." *Big Medicine From Six Nations*. Syracuse, NY: Syracuse University Press, 2007.

Wilson, Ivy, ed. *Whitman Noir: Black America and the Good Gray Poet*. Iowa City: University of Iowa Press, 2014.

Winks, Robin W. "The Making of a Fugitive Slave Narrative: Josiah Henson and Uncle Tom—A Case Study." In *The Slave's Narrative*, edited by Charles T. Davis and Henry Louis Gates Jr. Oxford: Oxford University Press, 1985.

Wondrich, David. "Ancient Mystery Revealed! The Real History (Maybe) of How the Cocktail Got Its Name." *Saveur* (January 14, 2016).

Zabel, Morton Dauwen, ed. *The Art of Travel: Scenes and Journeys in America, England, France and Italy from the Travel Writings of Henry James*. Garden City, NJ: Doubleday Anchor Books, 1958.

Index

American: customs, 58, 161n5; female beauty, 62; landscape, 93; readers, 161n5
antislavery, 167n10; novel, 77; societies, 75

Brooke, Rupert, 117–21

Canada's Act to Limit Slavery of 1793, 75
canals: Erie Canal, 11, 29–30, 42, 158n1; Welland Canal, 33
Cave of the Winds, 6, 71, 146
cholera, 28–30, 42
Civil War, American, 113
cocktail, 124–25
Cooper, James Fenimore, 123–26
copyright laws, 56–59, 64
Cusick, Col. Nicholas, 16, 17
Cusick, David, 10, 15–19, 168n1

Dawn Settlement, 79–80
de Charlevoix, Pierre Francois Xavier, 12
Dickens, Charles, 56–64, 123, 162n2, 163n8–9, 163n12
Dow, Charles Mason, 5–6
Doyle, Sir Arthur Conan, 127–32

Emerson, Ralph Waldo, 1–4, 151n6, 152n7

Falls, the: cultural and personal significance, as a symbol of, 5; illustration of, 97; ruin of, 143
Five Nations, constitution of, 111
Forsyth, William, 11, 154n9
Frankenstein, Godfrey, 99–100, 102–3
Free Niagara Movement, 141–42
Fugitive Slave Act, 75, 78, 87
Fuller, Margaret, 11, 19–26, 156n21, 156n24

Goat Island, 103, 110

Haudenosaunee Confederacy, 111
Hawthorne, Nathaniel, 42–49, 156n24, 160n4, 161n8
Hennepin, Fr. Louis, 9, 26, 97, 151n1–2, 161n1
Henson, Rev. Josiah, 76–83, 153n12
Hill, Isaac, 15–17
Howells, William Dean, 6, 97–106, 123
Hustler, Catherine "Kitty," 124–25
hydroelectric power, 143

indigenous: authors, 10; inhabitants, 9; lands, 13, 18, 149; material culture, 10; writers, 16
Iroquois, 12, 111; Catholic, 12–13, 155n8, 155n10
Irving, Washington, 28–32, 57–58, 97, 158n5–6, 158n12, 168n8

Jacket, Red, 16
James, Henry, 106–10, 142–43
Johnson, Dr. Paul L. S., 130

Lake Erie, 92–93
London, Jack, 132–40
Longfellow, Henry Wadsworth, 28, 38–40
Lumley, Arthur, xiii–xiv

Maid of the Mist, 68, 126
Mann, Horace, Jr., 34
McKenney, Thomas L., 17
Moore, Thomas, 41

narrative: captivity, 12–13. *See also* narratives
narratives: freedom, 75; slave, 75–76, 78
Niagara Falls: city of, 43; illustration of, xiii; literary story of, 9

Parker, Arthur Caswell, 111
picturesque, the, 27, 109, 143
Porter, Col. Peter A., 7
Porter, Gen. Peter B., 21–22

reading public, 2, 55

Sedgwick, Catharine Maria, 10–15, 28, 154n7, 155n10–13
Six Nations, 16–19, 168n3; Mohawk, 12, 17, 111, 156n4; Seneca, 16–18, 156n24, 156n28; Tuscarora, 15–18, 111, 146n24, 168n3
spiritualism, 127–31
Stowe, Harriet Beecher, 75–80, 165n6
sublime, 5, 19–21, 119; technological, 85, 143
Suspension Bridge, 63, 70, 85–88, 94, 151n5, 160n22, 167n5, 168n3

Table Rock, 11, 14, 21, 23, 46, 62, 116, 126, 163n12
technologies: mobility, 4; print, 55
Thoreau, Henry David, 32–37, 159n20
tourism, 52, 143, 152n9; industry, 10–12, 44–49; landscape, 5; rise of, 27; tourists, 11, 26–27, 43–44, 52, 65, 143–44, 152n9, 156n24. *See also* tourist traps
tourist traps, 119
travel: essays, 4, 44, 106–7, 142; narrative, 43, 65, 107, 149; sketches, 42; writing, 10, 64, 106–7, 119, 164n13
Trollope, Anthony, 97–98, 112–17
Tubman, Harriet, 86–92, 153n12, 156n3–57n6
Twain, Mark, 56, 64–73, 85, 153n12, 164n13–15

Underground Railroad, 43, 75, 156n23; Heritage Center, Niagara Falls, 5, 161n7

war: of words 143; markers of, 111
Wells, H. G., 142–48
Whitman, Walt, 92–96, 167n10
Wilde, Oscar, 5, 49–53, 65, 142, 161n9–62n10
Williams, Eleazar, 12
Williams, Eunice, 12
Williams, Ted, 112